Siddhartha

Hermann Hesse

About the Cover: Being dead (shown on the front cover) and being alive (shown on the back cover) always go hand in hand, but they are distinguished from each other just by a breath. Likewise, being awakened and being unawakened exist side by side, but they always remain apart from each other just by a thought.

—Siddhartha

Author: Hermann Hesse (1922)

English Translator: Sine Nomine (2015)

This English translation of *Siddhartha* is first printed in 2015 in the United States of America by CreateSpace at
7290 B Investment Drive
Charleston, SC 29418

Toll free: 1-866-308-6235

Siddhartha can be purchased either at Amazon.com or at
https://www.createspace.com/4819941

Library of Congress Control Number (LCCN): 2014909525

(ISBN-10): 1-4996-4562-7
(ISBN-13): 978-1-499-64562-0

This English translation of Hesse's *Siddhartha*, which can be purchased at Amazon.com or at https://www.createspace.com/4819941, is just the novel itself. This same translating version along with its insights that were presented by the Venerable Thích Nữ Trí Hải will be available under the title *Siddhartha and Its Insights*. The latter is more for those who are interested in how *Siddhartha* is seen through the lens of Buddhism.

For all comments and requests, please contact the copyright owner at:
sinenomine09@yahoo.com

TABLE OF CONTENTS

THE BRAHMIN'S SON

In the shade of the house, in the sunshine on the river bank by the boats, in the shade of the sallow wood, and in the shade of the fig tree, Siddhartha, the handsome Brahmin's son, grew up with his friend, Govinda. The sun browned his slender shoulders when he bathed at the holy ablutions and at the holy sacrifices on the river bank. Shadows risen up from profound thoughts passed across his eyes every time when he strolled in the mango grove, when he listened to his mother singing, when he concentrated on his father teaching, and when he dwelled on the learned men discussing. Siddhartha had already long taken part in the learned men's conversations, had engaged in debates with Govinda, and had practiced the arts of contemplation and meditation with him.

Already, he knew how to pronounce Om in silence—this word of words— to say it inwardly when breathing in and to say it outwardly when breathing out with all his soul while his brow radiated the glow of pure spirit. Already, he knew how to recognize Atman, an indestructible individual soul, within the depth of his being and how to cherish the feeling of one with the universe, the everlasting cosmic soul or the Brahman or the world soul.

There was happiness in his father's heart because of his son who was intelligent and thirsty for knowledge. The father envisaged his son growing up to be a great-learned man, a priest, and a prince among Brahmins.

There was pride in his mother's breast when she saw her son walking, sitting, and rising. Siddhartha—the strong, handsome boy with supple limbs— greeted his mother with complete grace.

Love stirred in the hearts of the young Brahmins' daughters when Siddhartha walked through the streets of the town with his lofty brow, with his king-like eyes, and with his slim figure.

Govinda, his friend, the Brahmin's son, loved him more than everyone else ever did. He loved Siddhartha's eyes and clear voice. He loved the way Siddhartha walked, his complete grace of movement. He loved everything that Siddhartha did and said. And above all, he loved Siddhartha's intellect; loved

Siddhartha's fine, ardent thought; loved Siddhartha's strong will; and loved Siddhartha's high vocation.

Govinda knew that Siddhartha would not become an ordinary Brahmin, a lazy sacrificial official, an avaricious dealer in magic sayings, a conceited worthless orator, a wicked sly priest, or just a good stupid sheep amongst a large herd.

No, and he, Govinda, himself, did not want to become any of those and did not want to become any Brahmin like tens of thousands of others of their kind. He wanted to follow Siddhartha—the beloved, magnificent one. If Siddhartha ever became a god and if he ever entered the All-Radiant, Govinda would then want to follow him as his friend, as his companion, as his servant, as his lance bearer, and as his shadow.

That was how everybody loved Siddhartha. He delighted everyone and made everyone happy, but he, himself, was not happy.

While wandering along the rosy paths of the fig garden and while sitting in contemplation under the bluish shade of the grove, Siddhartha was always beloved by all. While washing his limbs in the daily bath of atonement and while offering sacrifices in the depths of the shady mango wood with complete grace of manner, he was always a joy to all. However, there was yet no joy in his heart.

Illusions and restless thoughts—rising up from the flowing river, sparkling down from the twinkling stars, and emitting outwards from the sun's melting rays—crammed into his mind. Dreams and vain thoughts—rising from the smoke of the sacrifices, emanating from the verses of the Rig-Veda, and trickling through from the teachings of the old Brahmins—invaded his soul.

Siddhartha had begun to feel the seeds of discontent within him. He had also begun to recognize that the love of his father, the love of his mother, and the love of his friend, Govinda, could not always suffice to make him happy, to give him peace, to provide him with satisfaction, and to quench the thirst inside him.

Siddhartha began to suspect that his worthy father and his other teachers, the wise Brahmins, had already passed on to him the bulk and the best of their wisdom and believe that they already poured the sum total of their knowledge into his waiting vessel. However, his waiting vessel was not yet full; his intellect was not yet satisfied; his soul was not yet at peace; and his heart was not yet still.

The water used to perform ablutions was good, but the water was just the water. It could not wash sins away or relieve the distressed heart. The sacrifices and the supplications of the gods were excellent, but were they all? Did these sacrifices and the supplications give happiness?

What about the gods? Was it really Prajapati creating the world? Was it not Atman—He, himself, alone—who had created the universe? Were the gods not the forms that were created like transients and mortals, like you and me? And was it, therefore, good and right? And was it, therefore, sensible and worthwhile to offer sacrifices to the gods? To whom else should one offer sacrifices? And to whom else should one pay honor other than to Him—Atman, the only One?

Where was Atman to be found? Where did He dwell, and where did His eternal heartbeat if it was not within the *Self* in the everlasting innermost place that each person carried within him? But, where was this *Self*, and where was this everlasting innermost place? The *Self* was neither flesh nor bone, and the everlasting innermost place was neither in thought nor in consciousness. These were what the learned men taught Siddhartha. Where, then, was Atman?

To press towards the *Self*, towards Atman, was there any other way that was worth seeking? Nobody knew where the *Self* was; nobody could show the way—neither his father nor his teachers nor the learned men and nor the holy songs.

The Brahmins and their holy books knew everything, everything. They have gone deep into everything—the creation of the world and the origin of all things, including of speech, of food, of inhalation, of exhalation, of the arrangement of six roots of sensations, and of the acts of the gods. They knew an infinite number of things, but was it worthwhile knowing all these things if they did not know the one important thing, the only important thing?

Many verses of the holy books, especially the Upanishades of the Samaveda, spoke of this innermost place. It was written, "Your soul is the whole world." It was also written, "When a man is asleep, he penetrates deep into his innermost place and dwells in Atman." There was wonderful wisdom in these verses. All the knowledge of the wise sages was told here in the enchanting language, pure as the honey collected by the bees. No, this tremendous amount of knowledge, assembled and preserved by successive generations of the learned Brahmins, could not be easily despised.

However, where were the Brahmins; where were the priests; and where were the learned men who were successful not only in having this most profound knowledge but also in experiencing it? Where were the initiated people who could reach Atman in sleep and could retain it—not only in consciousness and in life every moment of the day but also in speech and in action everywhere?

Siddhartha knew many highly regarded Brahmins, especially his father— the holy one, the learned one, and the most venerable one. His father was worthy of admiration. His manner was quiet and noble. He lived a good life; his words were wise; and his fine, noble thoughts dwelt in his head, but, even he who knew so much, did he live in bliss? Was he at peace? Was he not also an insatiable seeker? Did he not continually go to the holy springs, go to the sacrifices, go to books, and go to the Brahmins' discourses with an unquenchable thirst?

Why did his father, the blameless one, have to wash away his sins and endeavor to cleanse himself anew each day? Was Atman, then, not within him? Was the source, then, not within his heart? Everyone had to find the source within one's own *Self* and had to possess it. Trying to find everything else was merely seeking random error, taking a detour, or plunging into confusion.

All these were Siddhartha's thoughts, were Siddhartha's longings, and were Siddhartha's sorrows.

Siddhartha often repeated to himself the words from one of the Chandogya-Upanishad. "In truth, the name of Brahman is Satyam. Indeed, those who know the real meaning behind this name will enter the heavenly world each day." This heavenly world seemed near, but never had he quite reached it and never had he quenched the final thirst. And among all the wise men whom he knew and whose teachings he enjoyed, no one could entirely enter the heavenly world, and no one could completely quench the eternal thirst.

"Govinda," said Siddhartha to his friend, "my friend, comes with me to the

Banyan tree. We will practice meditation."

They went to the Banyan tree and sat down, twenty paces apart. After Siddhartha sat down and was ready to pronounce the Om, he softly recited the verse,

"Om is the bow; the arrow is the soul,
Brahman is the arrow's goal
at which one aims unflinchingly."

After the customary time for the practice of meditation had passed, Govinda rose. It was now evening, which was time to perform the evening ablution. He called Siddhartha by his name, but he did not reply.

Siddhartha sat still and was completely absorbed. His eyes fixed on the horizon as if he directly stared at a distant goal. The tip of his tongue stuck out a little between his teeth, and he did not seem to be breathing. He sat as if he was lost in meditation and thinking about Om while his soul, like the arrow, headed directly to Brahman.

One day, a few Samanas passed through Siddhartha's town. As wandering ascetics, they were three thin, worn-out men who were neither old nor young. Their shoulders were bleeding and were covering with dust. They were practically naked, were scorched by the sun, were surrounded by a strange loneliness, and appeared in sharp contrast to the worldly men. They looked like hostile, lean jackals. Around them hovered an atmosphere of still passion, of fervent service, and of unpitying self-denial.

Later in the evening, after the hour of contemplation, Siddhartha told Govinda, "Tomorrow morning, my friend, Siddhartha is going to join the Samanas. He is going to become a Samana."

Govinda blanched as he heard these words and as he read the decision in his friend's determined face. This undeviating willpower of Siddhartha was like a released arrow from the bow. Govinda realized from the first glance at his friend's face that now it was beginning. Siddhartha was going his own way. Siddhartha's destiny was beginning to unfold itself, and so was Govinda's destiny. Govinda's face suddenly turned pale as a dried banana skin.

"Oh Siddhartha," Govinda stumbled over the words as his voice wavered, "will . . . will . . . will your father permit it?"

Siddhartha looked at his friend as if he, himself, was the one who just became awakened. As quick as lightning, he read not only Govinda's soul and Govinda's anxiety but also Govinda's resignation.

"We will not waste words, Govinda," said Siddhartha softly.

"Tomorrow at daybreak, I will begin the life of the Samanas. Let us not discuss it again."

Siddhartha went into the room where his father was sitting on a mat made of bast. He went up behind his father and remained standing there until his father felt his presence.

"Is it you, Siddhartha?" asked the Brahmin. "Then speak what is in your mind."

Siddhartha said, "With your permission, my dear father, I have come to tell you that I wish to leave your house tomorrow and join the ascetics. I wish to become a Samana. I trust my father will not object."

The Brahmin was silent for a long time. He remained silent so long that the stars passed across the small window and changed their design before the silence in the room was finally broken.

The son stood silent and motionless with his arms folded while the father, who was also silent and motionless, remained sitting on the mat. Now, the stars already passed across the sky . . .

The father then said, "It is not seemly for Brahmins to utter forceful and angry words, but there is displeasure in my heart. I would much prefer not to hear you make this request the second time."

The Brahmin rose slowly, but Siddhartha remained silent with folded arms.

"Why are you still waiting?" asked the father.

"You know why," answered Siddhartha.

The father, still with the displeasure in his heart, left the room and went to lie down on his bed.

As an hour passed by, and the Brahmin could not sleep. He rose, wandered up and down, and then left the house. He looked through the small window of the room and saw Siddhartha standing there with his arms folded, unmoving. He could see Siddhartha's pale robe shimmering. While his heart still troubled, he returned to his bed.

As another hour passed by, and the Brahmin still could not sleep. He, once again, rose and wandered up and down. He then left the house and saw the moon already rising high. He looked through the window. Siddhartha yet stood there unmoving, and his arms yet folded. The moon now shone on Siddhartha's bare shinbones. The father went back to bed while the trouble still lingered in his heart.

The Brahmin returned outside again after an hour and again after two hours. Looking through the window, he saw Siddhartha still standing there in the moonlight, in the starlight, and in the dark.

In silence, the Brahmin came back outside again, hour after hour. He looked into the room and still saw Siddhartha standing there unmoving. His heart now filled with anger, with anxiety, with fear, and with sorrow.

And in the last hour of the night, before daybreak, the father returned outside again, entered the room, and saw the youth still standing there. Siddhartha now seemed tall and looked like a stranger to him.

"Siddhartha," said the Brahmin, "why are you still waiting?"

"You know why."

"Will you go on standing and waiting until it is day, noon, and evening?"

"I will stand and wait."

"You will grow tired, Siddhartha."

"I will grow tired."

"You will fall asleep, Siddhartha."

"I will not fall asleep."

"You will die, Siddhartha."

"I will die."

"And would you rather die than obey your father?"

"Siddhartha has always obeyed his father."

"So you will give up your project?"

"Siddhartha will do what his father tells him."

The first light of the day entered the room. The Brahmin noticed that Siddhartha's knees were trembling slightly, but there was no tremble in Siddhartha's face. There was, however, a faraway look in Siddhartha's eyes. The father now realized that Siddhartha could no longer remain with him at home and that Siddhartha had already left him.

The father fondly placed his hand on Siddhartha's shoulder. "You will go into the forest," said the father, "and become a Samana. If you find bliss in the deep forest, please come back and teach it to me. On the contrary, if you find disillusionment, please also come back. We shall again offer sacrifices to the gods together. Now go, kiss your mother, and tell her where you are going. For me, however, it is time to go to the river and perform the first ablution."

The father dropped his hand from his son's shoulder and went out.

Siddhartha swayed as he tried to walk. While trying to control his balance, he bowed to his father and went to his mother to do what his father had told him.

As, with benumbed legs, Siddhartha slowly left the still sleeping town at daybreak, a crouching shadow emerged from the last hut and joined the pilgrim. It was Govinda.

"You have come," said Siddhartha and smiled.

"I have come," said Govinda.

Remark: Siddhartha plunged into the ascetic life with a heartfelt desire. He decided to leave all sacrifices and supplications of the gods behind, to go away from Prajapati, and to seek the *Self* in the everlasting innermost place in his own way.

CHAPTER 2

WITH THE SAMANAS

In the evening of that day, Siddhartha and Govinda caught up with the Samanas. They then offered their company and pledged their allegiance to the Samanas. They were accepted.

Siddhartha gave his clothes to a poor Brahmin whom he met on the road and only retained his loincloth and earth-colored unstitched cloak. He only ate once a day and never cooked food. He fasted fourteen days. He fasted twenty-eight days.

The flesh disappeared from his legs and from his cheeks. Strange dreams were reflected in his enlarged eyes. The nails grew long on his thin fingers, and a dry, bristly beard appeared on his chin. His glance became ice cold when he encountered women. His lips curled with contempt when he passed through a town of well-dressed people.

He saw businessmen trading, princes going to a hunt, mourners weeping over their dead, prostitutes offering themselves, doctors attending the sick, priests deciding what to sow for the day, lovers making love, and mothers soothing their children. None of them was worth a passing glance. Everything lied. Everything stank of lies. Happiness and beauty were all illusions of six roots of sensations. All were doomed to decay. The world tasted bitter. Life was a pain.

Siddhartha only had one single goal, and that was to become empty—empty of thirsts, empty of desires, empty of dreams, empty of pleasures, and empty of sorrows. He wanted to let the *Self* die. He wanted to let it no longer be the *Self* so that he could experience the peace of an emptied heart and could experience the pure soul. That was his goal. When the *Self* was conquered and destroyed, and when all passions and desires sank into silence, the last, the Dharmata, then had to manifest itself. The innermost of being—the great secret, which was not the *Self*—became awakened!

Silently, Siddhartha stood under the fierce sun's rays, blazed with smarts, flamed with pain, and filled with thirst. He stood until he no longer felt smart, pain, and thirst. Silently, he stood in the rain. The water was dripping from his hair onto his freezing shoulders, onto his freezing hips, and onto his freezing legs. The ascetic stood until his shoulders and his legs no longer froze, until they no longer had feelings, and until they no longer mobilized.

In silence, Siddhartha crouched among sharp thorns. Blood dripped from his smarting skin, and ulcers formed. He remained stiff and motionless until no more blood flowed, until no more prickling recognized, and until no more smarting perceived.

Next, Siddhartha sat upright and learned to save his breath. He managed to maintain his life with as little breathing as possible and with holding his breath for as long as possible. While breathing in, he learned to quiet his heartbeats and learned to lessen his heartbeats. He kept practicing until there were a very few and until there was hardly anymore.

Instructed by the eldest of the Samanas, Siddhartha practiced self-denial and meditation according to the Samana rules. A heron flew over the bamboo wood, and Siddhartha took the heron into his soul. He became a heron, flew over forest and mountains, felt the pangs of a heron hunger, ate fish, used heron language, and experienced the death of a heron.

In another time, a dead jackal lay on the sandy shore, and Siddhartha's soul slipped into its corpse. He became a dead jackal and remained lying dead on the shore. The carcass eventually swelled, stank, and decayed. Hyenas dismembered the rotten corpse and ate four legs. Vultures picked all the flesh and left behind a bare skeleton, which finally became dust particles mingled with the atmosphere. Siddhartha's soul, then, returned, died, bloated, decayed, turned into dust, and experienced the wretched course of the life cycle.

With a new thirst, Siddhartha waited for another experience coming along as if a hunter stood on a cliff looking directly down into a chasm where the life cycle ends, where no cause was needed, and where the painless eternity began.

Siddhartha killed his senses. He killed his memory. He slipped out of his *Self* in hundreds of thousands of different forms. He was animal, carcass, carrion, stone, wood, and even water. And after every time, he re-awakened. The sun still rose; the moon still shone; and he was still his own *Self.* All over again, he swung into the life cycle, felt thirsty, conquered thirst, and then felt new thirst

Siddhartha learned a great deal from the Samanas. He learned many ways of losing the *Self*. He travelled along the path of self-denial through intentionally enduring pain, through voluntarily accepting afflictions, through deliberately conquering anguish, through indefatigably fighting against hunger, through resolutely warding off thirst, and through unwaveringly overcoming fatigue.

He also travelled along the path of self-denial through wholeheartedly concentrating on meditation and through completely emptying all images in his mind. Along the path of self-denial and other paths, he did learn how to travel. He lost his *Self* a thousand times, and for days on end, he dwelt in no *Self* and in non-being. All these paths took him away from the *Self*, but in the end, they always brought him back to the *Self*.

Although Siddhartha fled from the *Self* a thousand times and dwelt in non-living things like carcass, carrion, stone, wood, and water, returning to the *Self* was inevitable. The hour at which he found himself returning to the *Self* was inevitable. In sunshine, in moonlight, in shadow, and in rain, Siddhartha, once again, dwelt in his *Self* and felt the torment of the onerous life cycle.

At Siddhartha's side was Govinda who lived as if he was Siddhartha's shadow. Govinda travelled along the same paths and made the same endeavors. They rarely conversed with each other except when they needed to exchange necessities involved their services and practices or when they went together through the villages in order to beg food for themselves and for their teachers.

"What do you think, Govinda?" Siddhartha asked at the beginning of one of the begging expeditions. "Do you think we are going any further? Have we reached our goal?"

Govinda replied, "We have learned, and we are still learning. You will become a great Samana, Siddhartha. You have learned every exercise quickly. The oldest Samana has often appraised you. Someday, you will be a holy man, Siddhartha."

Siddhartha said, "It does not appear so to me, my friend. Whatever I have, so far, learned from the Samanas, I could learn more quickly and easily in every inn, in every prostitute's quarter, with the carriers, and from dice players."

Govinda said, "Siddhartha must be joking. How could you have learned how to meditate, how to hold your breath, and how to remain imperturbable before hunger and pain from those wretches?"

Siddhartha softly replied as if he was talking to himself, "What is meditation? What is abandonment of the body? What is abstinence from food? What is regulation of breathing? Every single one of them is a temporary flight from the *Self* and a temporary escape from the torment of the *Self*. Each one of them is just a temporary palliative that help alleviate the pain and help mitigate follies of life. The driver of oxen makes the same temporary flight, exploits the same temporary escape mechanism, and takes the same kind of temporary drug when he drinks a few bowls of either rice wine or coconut milk in the inn. He then no longer feels his *Self* and no longer feels the pain in his life. That is how he experiences his temporary escape. While falling asleep over his bowl of rice-wine, he finds exactly what Siddhartha and Govinda find when they escape from their bodies by practicing long exercises and by dwelling in no *Self*."

Govinda said, "You speak thus, my friend, but deep down inside, you know that Siddhartha is no driver of oxen, and a Samana is no drunkard. The drinker, of course, can find a temporary escape and, of course, can find a short respite or a temporary rest; however, when he returns from the illusion, he finds everything as it was before. He has not grown any wiser; he has not gained any knowledge; and he has not climbed any higher on the ladder of experience."

Siddhartha answered with a smile on his face, "I do not know. I have never been a drunkard, but I, Siddhartha, can only find a short respite while exercising self-denial and practicing meditation. I am still remote from wisdom and still remote from salvation; thus, I feel as if I was like a child in the womb. These happenings, Govinda, I do know. I know them for sure."

On another occasion, when Siddhartha left the wood with Govinda in order to beg for food for their brothers and their teachers, Siddhartha began the conversation and asked, "Well, Govinda, are we on the right road? Are we gaining any additional knowledge? Are we approaching salvation? Or are we perhaps going in circles of birth and death, but we are thinking that we are seeking a way to escape from those cycles?"

Govinda said, "We have learned much, Siddhartha. There still remains much to learn. We are not going in circles. We are going upwards. The path is more like an upward spiral, and we have already passed through many loops."

Siddhartha asked, "How old do you think our oldest Samana, our worthy teacher, is?"

Govinda said, "At the most, I think the eldest could be about sixty years old."

Siddhartha recapitulated with a sarcastic tone of voice, "He is sixty years old and still has not yet attained nirvana. He will be seventy and then eighty years old. You and I, we shall also grow old. We shall be as old as he is. Like him, we can do exercises, can fast, and can meditate, but we will not attain nirvana. Neither he nor we will attain nirvana. Govinda, amongst all Samanas, I believe that perhaps, no one will attain nirvana. We find consolations. We learn simple tricks to deceive ourselves, but the essential thing—the way—we cannot learn."

"Do not utter such dreadful words, Siddhartha," said Govinda. "How could it be that among so many learned men, among so many worthy Brahmins, among so many abstinent Samanas, among so many faithful seekers, among so many dedicated followers, and among so many holy men who devote their time and effort to their spiritual lives, no one will find the right way?"

Siddhartha, however, said in a soft voice which contained as much grief as mockery and as much dejection as jesting, "Soon, Govinda, your friend will leave the path of the Samanas along which he has travelled with you so long. I suffer thirst, Govinda, and on this long Samana path, my thirst has not grown any less. I have always thirsted for knowledge, but by the same token, I have always been full of questions. Year after year, I have questioned the faithful Brahmins. Year after year, I have questioned the holy Vedas. Perhaps, Govinda, it would have been equally good, equally clever, and equally holy if I had questioned rhinoceros or chimpanzees. I have spent a long time and have wasted a lot of time, but I still have not yet finished learning one thing, Govinda. What is the one thing that I should have learned a long time ago, but I did not? That one thing is 'One can learn nothing'. For this reason, I believe that in the essence of everything, there is something we just can never learn. There is, Govinda, my friend, only knowledge that is everywhere, and that knowledge is the Brahman. It is in you, in me, and in every living creature. I am now beginning to believe in the fact that this knowledge has no worse enemy than the man of knowledge and no worse foe than the man of learning."

Thereupon, Govinda stopped walking, stood still on the road, raised his hands, and grieved, "Siddhartha, do not distress your friend with such talk. Truly, your words trouble me. Think, Siddhartha. Think about the meanings of our holy prayers, think about the venerableness of the Brahmins, and think about the holiness of the Samanas . . . If, as you say, one can learn nothing, then there is no learning, and nothing has meaning. If what you said were true, Siddhartha, what would everything in this world become? If what you said were true, who would be holy on earth? If what you said were true, what would be precious? And if what you said were true, which would be sacred?"

Under the breath, Govinda murmured a verse from one of the Upanishad to himself,

> "He, whose reflective pure spirit sinks into the Brahman,
>   Knows bliss that cannot be expressed in words."

Siddhartha was silent. He dwelt long on the words, which Govinda just uttered.

"Yes . . ." Siddhartha stood with his head bowed and mumbled to himself, ". . . What remains from all things that seem holy to us? What remains from all things that seem sacred to us? What remains? What remains from all things that should be preserved?" He shook his head.

When both youths had lived with the Samanas and had shared their practice with each other for about three years, they heard a rumor, a report, from many sources. Someone, named Gotama, the Illustrious One, the Buddha, had appeared. He had conquered all sorrows of the world in himself and had brought his cycle of life and death to a standstill. He wandered everywhere in the country to preach. Many people surrounded him, listened to him, swore their allegiance to him, and followed him as his disciples. Gotama owned no possession, was homeless, had no wife, and wore the yellow cloak of an ascetic, but with a lofty brow and with a holy appearance, Brahmins and princes bowed before him and became his pupils.

This report, this rumor, this tale was first heard here and there, but it was then spread everywhere. The Brahmins talked about it in the town, and the

Samanas talked about it in the forest. The name of Gotama, the Buddha, eventually reached the ears of the young men. The rumor spoke of both, well spoken and ill spoken. One time was in praise, but another time was in scorn.

Just as when the country was ravaged by an outbreak of the plague, a rumor arose. There was a man, a wise man, a learned man, whose words and breath were sufficient to heal the afflicted.

As the report travelled across the country and as everyone spoke about it, a good many believed in it, but in contrast, a good many others doubted it. Among those who believed in it, many immediately went on their way to seek the wise man, the benefactor.

In a manner as such, the good report about Gotama, the Buddha, the wise man from the family of Sakya, travelled through the country. "He possesses great knowledge;" said the believers, "he remembers his former lives. He has already attained nirvana and will never return to the cycles of life and death. He plunges no more into the troubled stream of forms."

Many wonderful and incredible things were also reported about him, "He has performed wonders, has conquered the devil, and has spoken with the gods." His enemies and his doubters, however, said that this Gotama was an idle fraud. He passed his days in high living, scorned the sacrifices, was unlearned, and knew neither mindfulness meditation exercises nor practices of mortification of the flesh.

The rumors about the Buddha, indeed, had the power to grab people's attention. It appeared as if there was magic in these reports. The world was sick, and life was difficult; thus, it seemed that a new hope flashed here and there. It also seemed that a holy messenger brought a soothing comfort full of fine promises. Everywhere, there were the rumors about the Buddha. Young men all over India listened, felt a longing, and waited for a new hope. Everywhere in towns and in villages, the Brahmans' sons warmly greeted pilgrims and strangers who brought news of him, the Illustrious One, the Sakyamuni, to them.

The rumors eventually reached the Samanas in the forest where Siddhartha and Govinda dwelt. A little at a time, both young Samanas learned about the rumors. Every little report they heard was heavy with hope, but it was also heavy with doubt. The two rarely spoke about these rumors because the eldest

Samana was no friend of these rumors.

The eldest Samana heard that in the past, this alleged Buddha was an ascetic and lived in the wood, but later on, he turned to high living and then took pleasure in the material world. Thus, the eldest Samana held no high opinion for this Gotama.

"Siddhartha," Govinda once said to his friend, "This morning, when I was in the village, a Brahmin invited me to enter his house. While I was in his house, I met his son who just came back from Magadha. His son told me that he had seen the Buddha walking with his own eyes and had heard the Buddha preaching with his own ears. Truly, I was filled with longing and thought, 'I wish that both Siddhartha and I may live to see the day when we both can meet the Buddha and can hear the teachings from the lips of the Perfected One.' My friend, shall we also go to that place to listen to the teachings from the lips of the Buddha?"

Siddhartha said, "I always thought that Govinda would remain with the Samanas. I also always believed that my friend would live up to sixty or even seventy years old and would still want to practice secret arts and secret exercises taught by the Samanas. Oh, how little did I know Govinda! How little did I know what was in his heart! Now, my dear friend, you wish to strike a new path. You wish to go to hear the Buddha's teachings."

Govinda said, "It gives you pleasure to mock me, doesn't it? It does not matter if you do, Siddhartha. How is it about you? Do you not also feel a longing and a desire to hear his teachings? And did you not once tell me, 'I will not travel the path of the Samanas much longer.'?"

Siddhartha burst out laughing aloud in such a way that his voice expressed a shade of sorrow and a shade of mockery. He said, "Well spoken. You have spoken very well, Govinda. You have remembered well what I told you, but you should also remember what else I told you, 'I have become distrustful of teachings and learning's and have had very little faith in words that come to us from teachers.' However, very well, my friend, I am ready to hear new teachings from the lips of the Buddha even though, deep down in my heart, I still believe that we have already tasted the best fruits of teachings."

Govinda replied, "I am delighted that you are agreed. But tell me, my friend, how could the teachings of Gotama be among the best fruits, or how could his teachings reveal the most precious fruit before we even have a chance to listen to him?"

Siddhartha said, "Let us first enjoy this fruit and await forthcoming ones, Govinda. The first yet the best fruit we have already been indebted to Gotama is the fact that he has enticed us to depart from the Samanas! Whether there are still other best fruits or precious fruits or not, let us patiently wait and see."

On the same day, Siddhartha informed the eldest Samana of their decision to leave him. He spoke to the old Samana with a polite and modest manner, which was completely appropriate for a young man and for a student. The old man, however, became angry after he learned that both young men wished to leave him. He then raised his voice and scolded them strongly.

Govinda was taken aback, but Siddhartha, in a calm demeanor, put his lips to Govinda's ear and whispered, "Now, I will show the old man that I have learned something from him."

Siddhartha stepped forward and stood near the old Samana. With his mind intent, he looked into the old Samana's eyes and held the old Samana with his look. In silence, he hypnotized the old Samana, made the old Samana mute, conquered the old Samana's will, and commanded the old Samana to do what he wished. The old Samana became silent; his eyes took on an absent expression; his will became crippled; and his arms hang down. He was, indeed, completely powerless under Siddhartha's spell. Siddhartha's thoughts utterly conquered the old Samana's thoughts; thus, the old Samana had to perform what Siddhartha commanded him. In this hypnotized state, the old Samana continued bowing several times. He finally gave his blessings to the young men and stammered his wishes for a good journey. Siddhartha and Govinda thanked him for his good wishes, returned his bow, and departed.

On the way, Govinda said, "Siddhartha, you have learned more from the Samanas than I am aware. It is difficult, very difficult to hypnotize an old Samana, but you successfully did it. In truth, if you stayed there, you would have soon learned how to walk on water."

"I have no desire to walk on water," said Siddhartha. "Let the old Samanas satisfy themselves with such arts!"

Remark: Siddhartha's first awakening—Asceticism offered him no wisdom.

CHAPTER 3

GOTAMA

In the town of Savathi, every child knew the name of the illustrious Buddha, and every house was ready to fill the alms bowls of Gotama's silently begging disciples. Near the town was Gotama's favorite adobe, the Jetavana Grove, which the rich merchant Anathapindika, a great devotee of the Illustrious One, presented it to him and his followers.

The two young ascetics, in their search for Gotama's adobe, were directed to this district. On their arrival to Savathi, food was offered to them immediately at the first house in front of whose door they stood silently begging. They partook of food, and Siddhartha asked the woman who handed him the food, "Good day lady, we would very much like to know where the Buddha, the Illustrious One, dwells for we are two Samanas from the forest. We would like to meet the Perfect One and to hear the teachings from his own lips."

The woman said, "You come to the right place, O Samanas from the forest. The Illustrious One sojourns in Jetavana, in the garden presented to him by Anathapindika. You may spend the night there, the pilgrims, for there is enough room for numerous people who flock there to hear the teachings from his lips."

Govinda rejoiced and happily said, "Ah, then we have reached our destination, and our journey is almost at an end. However, tell us, mother of pilgrims, do you know the Buddha? Have you seen him with your own eyes?"

The woman said, "I have seen the Illustrious One many times. Many days, I have seen him silently walking through the streets, in a yellow cloak, silently holding out his alms bowl at the front doors of the houses, and silently returning to the Jetavana Grove with his filled bowl."

Govinda listened enchanted. He wanted to ask many more questions and to hear much more, but Siddhartha reminded him that it was time to go. They both expressed their thanks and departed. Now, it was no longer necessary for them to inquire the way to the grove for quite a number of pilgrims and monks from Gotama's followers were on their way to Jetavana. Even after the young Samanas arrived at the grove at night, there were still continual new arrivals. There was a stir of voices from the pilgrims requesting to obtain shelter. The two Samanas, who were used to life in the forest, quickly and quietly found shelter and stayed there until the morning.

At sunrise, they were astounded to see the large number of disciples, believers, and curious people who had spent the night there. Monks in yellow robes wandered along all the paths in the magnificent grove. Here and there, a number of other monks sat under the shades of the trees, either lost in meditation or engaged in spiritual talks. The shady garden was like a town swarming with bees. Most of the monks departed from the grove with their alms bowls in order to beg for food for their midday meal, the only one of the day. Even the Buddha himself, he also went begging in the morning.

Siddhartha saw the Buddha and recognized him immediately. It was as if God pointed the Buddha out to him. He saw the Buddha who, like everyone else in a yellow cowl, bore an alms bowl and quietly left the grove.

"Look!" said Siddhartha softly to Govinda. "That is the Buddha."

Govinda looked attentively at the monk in the yellow cowl—a simple monk who could not be distinguished in any way from the hundreds of other monks, but Govinda also recognized him immediately. "Yes, it was he," whispered Govinda.

They both followed the Buddha and gazed at him with veneration. The Buddha went quietly on his way and lost in his thoughts. His peaceful countenance was neither happy nor sad. He seemed to be smiling gently inwardly. With a secret joy in his heart, his gentle smile was not any different from that of a healthy child. He walked along in silence and in peace. He wore his yellow gown and walked along the path. He looked exactly like other monks, but his face, his steps, and the way he carried himself were completely different from those of other monks. His peaceful downward glance, his peaceful downward hanging hand, and every finger of his hand all spoke of peace and spoke of completeness. He walked as if he sought nothing, requested nothing, and imitated no one. Every one of his fingers reflected a continuous tranquility, an unfading light, and an invulnerable peace.

Just like that, Gotama wandered into the town to beg for alms. The two

Samanas recognized him only by his complete peacefulness of demeanor and by his stillness of movement in which there were no yearning, no seeking, no presence of willpower, and no effort. All in him were only light and peace.

"Today, we will hear the teachings from his own lips," said Govinda.

Siddhartha did not reply. He was not very curious about the teachings because he did not think they would bring him anything new. He, as well as Govinda, had heard quintessence's of the Buddha's teachings even though they only heard from the second-hand and the third-hand reports. However, Siddhartha looked attentively at Gotama's head, at Gotama's shoulders, at Gotama's feet, and at Gotama's still, downward hanging-hands. It seemed to Siddhartha that every joint of every finger of Gotama' hand contained knowledge. Each one of them spoke; each one of them breathed; and each one of them radiated truth. This man, this Buddha, this Illustrious One was truly a holy man to his fingertips. Never had Siddhartha esteemed a man so much. Never had he loved a man so much.

The two young Samanas followed the Buddha into the town and returned to the grove in silence. They, themselves, intended to abstain from food that day. They watched Gotama return and watched him take his meal in the circle of his disciples. What he ate, indeed, would not satisfy a bird. Shortly after, they watched him withdraw to the shade of the mango tree.

In the evening, when the heat abated, and when everyone in the camp woke up, they all gathered to listen to the Buddha preaching. They heard his voice that was so perfect, so calm, so gentle, and so peaceful. Gotama talked about suffering, the origin of suffering, and the cessation of suffering. Life was pain, and the world was full of suffering, but the paths leading to the cessation of suffering had been found. There was salvation for those who followed the teachings of the Buddha.

The Illustrious One spoke in a soft but firm voice. He taught everyone the four noble truths, including the noble eightfold path which was the ways leading to the cessation of suffering. Besides using this gradual approach, he patiently extended his teaching to cover the usual method in which he exploited examples and repetitions for emphasis. Clearly and quietly, his voice was genuinely carried to his listeners. The voice was so distinctive that it was like the light from the sun and like the stars of heaven.

When the Buddha finished his teachings, it already ran into the night. Many pilgrims came forward and asked to be accepted into the community. The Buddha accepted them all and said, "You have listened well to the teachings. Join us then and walk in bliss. Join us and put an end to suffering."

Govinda, the shy one, also stepped forward and said, "I also wish to pay my allegiance to the Illustrious One and his teachings." He asked to be taken into the community and was accepted.

As soon as the Buddha withdrew for the night, Govinda turned to Siddhartha and eagerly said, "Siddhartha, it is not my place to reproach you. We both listened to the Illustrious One, and we both heard his teachings. Govinda attentively listened to the teachings and accepted them, but you, my dear friend, will you not also tread on the path of salvation? What holds you up? What are you waiting for?"

When Siddhartha heard Govinda's words, he suddenly jolted back to reality. It was as if he just woke up from a sleep. He then looked at Govinda's face for a long time. With no mockery in his voice, he spoke softly, "Govinda, my friend, you have taken the step. You have chosen your path. You have always been my friend, Govinda, and you have always gone a step behind me. Often, I have thought, 'Will Govinda ever, from his own conviction, take a step without me? Will Govinda ever, with his own confidence, take a step without me?' Now, you are a man, and you have chosen your own path. May you go along it all the way to the end, my friend! May you find salvation, Govinda!"

Govinda, who did not yet fully understanding, repeated his question impatiently, "Speak, my dear friend, say that you will also not do anything else other than swear your allegiance to the Buddha."

Siddhartha placed his hand on Govinda's shoulder, "You have heard my blessing, Govinda. I repeat it. May you travel this path all the way to the end! May you find salvation!"

At this very moment, Govinda realized that his friend was going to leave him, and he began to weep, "Oh Siddhartha . . ." Govinda sobbed his heart out.

Siddhartha kindly comforted him, "Govinda, do not forget that you now belong to the Buddha's holy men. You have renounced your home and your parents. You have renounced your origin and your property. You have renounced your will and your friendship. That is what the teachings preach; that is what the Illustrious One wishes; and that is what your heart desires. Tomorrow, Govinda, I will leave you."

As the night closed in, the two young friends wandered through the woods for a long time. They then lay down on the ground for quite a while, but neither of them could sleep. Govinda pressed Siddhartha again and again to tell him the reason that made his friend did not want to follow the Buddha's teachings and to tell him the flaw that his friend found in those teachings. Regardless of how many times Govinda insisted, Siddhartha waved him off every time, "Be at peace, Govinda. The Illustrious One's teachings are very good. How could I find any flaw in them?"

Early in the morning on the following day, one of the Buddha's followers, one of his oldest monks, went through the grove. He called to him all the new people who sworn their allegiance to the teachings yesterday evening so as to give them the yellow robe and to instruct them in the first teachings along with the duties of their order. Thereupon, Govinda tore himself away from all new monks, embraced the friend of his youth one last time before putting on the monk's robe, and then followed the eldest monks.

Siddhartha wandered through the grove deep in thought. There he met Gotama, the Illustrious One. As Siddhartha greeted the Buddha respectfully and found the peaceful gaze full of goodness in the Buddha's eyes, he plucked up his courage and asked the Illustrious One for the permission to speak to him. Silently, the Illustrious One nodded his head to indicate the permission granted.

Siddhartha said, "Yesterday, O Illustrious One, I had the pleasure of listening to your wonderful teachings. I came from afar with my friend to listen to you, and now my friend will remain with you. He has sworn his allegiance to you. I will, however, continue my pilgrimage anew."

"As you wish, my dear one!" said the Illustrious One politely.

"My words are perhaps too bold," continued Siddhartha, "but I do not wish to leave the Illustrious One without sincerely communicating my thoughts to him. Will the Illustrious One listen to me a little longer?"

Silently, the Buddha nodded his consent.

Siddhartha said, "O Illustrious One, in one thing above all, have I admired your teachings. Everything is completely clear and proved. You show the world as a complete, unbroken chain, an eternal chain, linked together by cause and effect. Never has the universe been presented so clearly, and never has the universe been demonstrated so irrefutably. Surely, every Brahmin's heart must beat more quickly when, through your teachings, he looks at the world as if it is a close synchronization—completely coherent, free of loophole, clear as a crystal, not dependent on chance, and not dependent on the gods. Whether the world is good or evil, whether life, itself, is painful or pleasurable, and whether subsistence is uncertain or not, it may be possible that none of them is important. However, the unity of the world, the coherence of all events, the interrelation among all things, the embrace of the big and the small from the same stream, the law of cause and effect, and the inevitability of birth and death are all clearly shone from your exalted teachings, O Perfect One. Nevertheless, according to your teachings, the unity and the logical consequence of all things have a small crack. Through this one small crack, there is something strange streaming into the world of unity. This something is new. This something was not there before, and it can neither be demonstrated nor be proved. This whole notion is your doctrine of rising above the world and is your doctrine of salvation. With this small crack, through this small fracture, the eternal universal law, however, eventually breaks down again. I beg your pardon for raising this objection."

In serenity, Gotama quietly listened. Now with kindness and politeness in a clear voice, the Perfect One spoke, "You have listened well to the teachings, O Brahmin's son, and it is very good that you have thought so deeply about them. You have found a flaw, but I wish you would carefully think about it again. Let me warn you, the young Samana who is thirsty for knowledge. You should stay away from the thicket of opinions and excuse yourself from the conflict of words. Opinions mean nothing. They may be beautiful, but they may also be ugly. They may be clever, but they may also be foolish. Thus, everyone can embrace them or reject them at his own will. The teachings, which you heard yesterday, however, are not my opinions, and their goals are not to explain the world to those who are thirsty for knowledge. Their goals are quite different. Their goals are to provide salvation to those who suffer. This is what Gotama teaches, nothing else."

"May I ask that you are not angry at me, O Illustrious One," said the young

Samana. "I did not mean to talk to you like so to quarrel with you about words. You are right when you assert that opinions simply mean nothing, but may I say one more thing? Never have I doubted you for one moment. I have never once doubted that you are the Buddha and that you have reached the highest level of enlightenment that so many thousands of Brahmins and Brahmins' sons are striving to reach. You have attained enlightenment through your own seeking, in your own way, through your own thoughts, through your own meditation practice, through your own knowledge, and through your own wisdom. You said that you have learned nothing through teachings, and because of what you said, O Illustrious One, so I think that nobody will find salvation through teachings. To anybody, O Illustrious One, can you communicate in words and demonstrate through teachings what happened to you at the hour of your enlightenment? The teachings of the enlightened Buddha embrace much and teach much, including how to live righteously and how to avoid evil. However, there is one thing that your comprehensible, clear, and worthy teaching does not contain. It does not contain the secret of what the Illustrious One, himself, experienced at that particular hour. You are, alone, the only one among hundreds of thousands knowing about that special moment. This is what I thought and realized when I heard your teachings. This is why I am going on my way. I am neither going to seek another doctrine nor going to seek a better doctrine for I know there is none. I, however, am going on my way because I want to leave all doctrines, to go away from all teachers, and to reach my goal by myself or to die alone. But I will often remember this day, O Illustrious One, and will often remember this hour—the hour when my eyes beheld a holy man."

The Buddha's eyes were lowered, and his unfathomable face expressed a complete equanimity. "I hope you are not mistaken in your reasoning," said the Illustrious One slowly. "May you reach your goal! However, tell me, have you seen many holy men and how many disciples who have gathered around me and have sworn their allegiance to my teachings? Do you, O Samana from afar, think that it would be better if all of them relinquished the teachings and returned to the life of the world filled with lustful desires?"

"This thought never occurred to me," uttered Siddhartha distinctly. "May they all follow the teachings! May they all reach their goal! It is not my place to judge another life. My judgment must only be for myself. Only for myself alone must I chose, and must I reject. We are the Samanas who seek liberation from the *Self*, O Illustrious One. If I were one of your followers, I fear that it would just only be on the surface and fear that I would deceive myself. What might happen is that it looks as if I was at peace and attained salvation from the *Self* while, in truth, the *Self* continues to live and continues to grow because it is transformed into your teachings, into my allegiance to you, into my love for you, and into my affection for the community of the monks."

With imperturbable brightness and with friendliness, the Buddha looked steadily at the young Samana while maintaining the half smiling. With this barely visible gesture of the Buddha, Siddhartha assumed that the Buddha wished to dismiss him.

"You are very clever, O Samana," said the Illustrious One. "You know how to speak cleverly, my friend. Be on your guard against too much cleverness!"

The Buddha walked away, but his look and his half-smile remained imprinted on Siddhartha's memory forever.

Siddhartha indistinctly spoke to himself, "I have never seen a man who looks, smiles, sits, and walks like that." He then continued, "I, myself, would very much like to look, to smile, to sit, and to walk like him. How free is he! How worthy is he! How restrained is he! How candid is he! How childlike is he! How mysterious is he! Only can a man who has conquered his *Self* look and can walk like that. So as to be like him, I will conquer my *Self*."

"I have seen one man, one man only," murmured Siddhartha, "before whom I must lower my eyes. I will never lower my eyes before another man. No other teaching will attract me since this man's teachings have done so. The Buddha has robbed me. Indeed, the Buddha has robbed me, but he has given me something of greater value in return. The Buddha has robbed me of my friend, Govinda, who previously believed in me but now believes in him. The Buddha has deprived me of my friend, Govinda, who was once my shadow but now becomes his shadow. However, the Buddha has given me Siddhartha, myself."

Siddhartha smiled pleasantly and moved on . . .

Remark: Siddhartha's second awakening—No one will find salvation through teachings.

CHAPTER 4

AWAKENING

As Siddhartha left the grove in which the Buddha, the Perfected One, remained, and in which Govinda, the friend of his youth, remained, he felt as if he left his former life behind him, in the grove, as well. When Siddhartha slowly went on his way, his mind was full of these thoughts.

He reflected deeply on why and on how he arrived at the decision to leave the grove. Until these feelings completely overwhelmed him, he reached the point where he recognized causes. It seemed to him that recognizing causes was simply thinking about thought. Through thoughts alone, feelings, instead of being lost in time, became knowledge, became real, and began to mature.

While walking along the way, he realized that he was no longer a youth. Rather, he was now a man. He also realized that something just left him. It was as if an old skin of a snake just left it. He felt that something that had accompanied him right through his youth and had been a part of him was no longer in him. What was that something if it was not the desire to have teachers in order to listen to their teachings? He left the last teacher whom he had met at the grove even though this last teacher was the greatest and wisest one—the holiest, the Buddha. He had to leave this teacher because he could not accept his teachings.

Slowly, the thinker went on his way and conversed with himself, "What is it that you wanted to learn from the teachers and from their teachings? Although they have taught you much, what is it that they could not to teach you?" After a deep, long contemplation, he answered his own question, "It is the *Self* whose character and nature are what I wished to learn. I want to escape from the *Self* and want to conquer it, but I cannot. Until now, all I have been capable of doing are to deceive it, to run away from it, and to hide from it. Truly, nothing in the universe has occupied my mind as much as the *Self* has. Oh, this riddle—that I live, that I exist, that I am one, that I am part of the universe, that I am separated, that I am different from everybody else, and that I am Siddhartha . . . Really, nothing in the universe about which do I know less than about my own *Self*!"

While being gripped by this thought, the thinker slowly w; but suddenly, he stood still because another thought, which ju one, immediately followed.

"What a clear thought!" murmured Siddhartha. "The reason that I know nothing about myself, that the Samana wanders aimlessly in a strange land by himself, and that Siddhartha remains alien to his own *Self* is due to one thing, one single thing—I am afraid of myself, the Samana is trying to reject himself, and Siddhartha is fleeing from his own *Self*."

Siddhartha sank deeply in thought, "I am seeking Atman [or the *Self*] and Brahman [or the *Great Self*]. The Samana is yearning to destroy himself. Siddhartha is craving to escape from himself. After all, everything boils down to one goal, and that is to find the nucleus of all things in the unknown innermost. However, while trying to locate the nucleus of all things, including Brahman, Atman, Life, the Divine, and the Absolute, I have lost myself along the way."

As Siddhartha looked up and gazed longingly at everything around him, a smile crept over his face. He felt that a strong feeling of awakening from a long dream spread right through his being. Immediately, he walked on again— walked quickly like a man who knew what he had to do.

"Yes," Siddhartha spoke softly and breathed deeply, "I will no longer try to escape from Siddhartha. I will no longer devote my thoughts to Atman. I will no longer give myself over to the sorrows of the world. I will no longer mutilate this body and destroy my *Self* in order to find a secret hidden behind the ruins. I will no longer study Yoga-Veda, Atharva-Veda, asceticism, and all other teachings. From now on, I will be my own teacher. I will be my own pupil. I will learn from myself the secret of Siddhartha."

Siddhartha looked around him as if he saw the world for the first time. The world was beautiful, strange, and mysterious. Here was blue; here was yellow; and here was green. Here were the sky and the river. Here were the wood and the mountain. All were beautiful. All were mysterious. All were enchanting. In the midst of everything, he, Siddhartha, the awakened one, was on the way to himself. All these things—the blue, the yellow, the green, the sky, the river, the wood, and the mountain, for the first time, passed through Siddhartha's eyes. They were no longer the magic's of Mara. They were no longer the ory veils of Maya. They were no longer the meaningless diversities of the world of appearances that were despised by deep-thinking Brahmins who scorned diversities but sought unity. River was a river, and the blue was blue. If a sacred unity, the One, the Divine, in Siddhartha secretly lived in the river and in the blue, it was just the divine art and the intention that revealed the coexistence of the river, of the colors, and of Siddhartha. Meaning and reality were not hidden somewhere behind things, but rather, they were within things, within everything in the universe.

"How deaf and how stupid I have been!" he walked on quickly with a secret smile but appeared to sink deeply in thoughts. "When a person reads something which he wishes to study, he does not despise its letters, does not deride its punctuation marks, does not call it an illusion, does not regard it as a chance, and does not consider it as a worthless shell. On the contrary, he reads it, studies it, and loves it—letter by letter, word by word, and sentence by sentence. I, conversely, who wished to read the book of the world and the book of my own nature, did take the liberty to despise the letters and to ridicule the signs. I called the world of appearances illusion, and I called my eyes and tongue chances. Now, everything is over. I have awakened. I have, indeed, awakened and have just been born today."

As these thoughts passed through Siddhartha's mind, he suddenly stopped and stood still for it was as if a snake lay in his path.

Then all of a sudden, he realized something clearly. He talked to himself, "Siddhartha who is now the awakened one or the newly born one must begin his life completely afresh. This morning, when Siddhartha left the Jetavana Grove—the grove of the Illustrious One who has already been awakened and has already been on the way to Him, it was Siddhartha's intention and seemed to be natural for him to return to the home of his parents and to stay with them after living the ascetic life for several years. Now, however, in the moment when he stood still as if a snake lay in his path, he also realized something else. He whispered as the thought came to his mind, "I am no longer who I was; I am no longer an ascetic; I am no longer a priest; and I am no longer a Brahmin. Then what shall I do at home with my father and my mother? Shall I study? Shall I offer sacrifices? Shall I practice meditation? No, all of these are now over for me."

As Siddhartha remained standing still for a long moment, an icy chill stole over him. He shivered inwardly like a small animal, like a tiny bird, and like a little rabbit when he realized how alone he was. He had been homeless for years, but he never once experienced a lonely feeling. He now, however, felt it. In the past, even when he was in the deepest meditation, he was still his father's son, was still a Brahmin of a high social standing, and was still a religious man. Now, he was only Siddhartha, the awakened one. Other than these two, he was no one else.

He breathed in deeply, and for a moment, he shuddered. Nobody was alone as he was. He was no longer a noble man, belonging to any aristocracy. He was no longer an artisan belonging to any guild. He found no refuge, had no place to go, shared his life with nobody, and spoke the same language with no one. He was no longer a Brahmin, sharing the life of the Brahmins. He was no longer an ascetic, belonging to the Samanas.

Even the most secluded hermit in the woods, he was not the only one and felt alone for he belonged to a class of people. Govinda had become a monk, and thousands of monks were his brothers who wore the exact same gown as his gown, shared the exact same beliefs with his beliefs, and spoke the exact same language as his language.

How about Siddhartha? Where would he belong? Whose life would he share? Whose language would he speak?

At this very moment, when the world around him melted away, and when he stood alone like a star in the sky, he was completely overwhelmed by a feeling of icy despair. However, he was more firm and determined than he ever was. This icy chill of despair was the last shudder before he became awakened and was the last pain before he became newly born.

Immediately, he moved on again. He walked quickly and impatiently. He no longer wished to head homewards, no longer wished to return to his father, and no longer wished to look backwards.

Remark: Siddhartha, once again, plunged into the worldly life with a heartfelt desire. He decided to leave all doctrines behind, to go away from all teachers, and to reach his goal by himself.

PART 2: CHAPTER 5

KAMALA

Siddhartha learned something new on every step of his path because the universe was transformed and because he was enthralled. He saw the sun rising over the forest and mountains and saw the sun setting behind the distant palm shore.

At night, he saw the stars arranging into constellations in the sky and saw the sickle-shaped moon floating like a boat in the blue. During the day, he saw trees, stars, animals, clouds, rainbows, rocks, caves, weeds, flowers, brooks, rivers, sparkles of dew on flowering bushes in the morning, and distant high mountains in pale blue. He listened to the birds singing, listened to the bees humming, and saw the wind blowing gently across rice fields. All of them that appeared in various colors and existed in thousands of different forms had always been there.

The sun and the moon had always shone; the rivers had always flowed; and the bees had always hummed, but in the past, to Siddhartha, they were nothing but fleeting and illusive veils before his eyes. He regarded them with distrust, expressed strong disapproval of them, and ostracized them from his thoughts because none of them was the reality, and because the reality lay on the other side of the visible. Now, however, his eyes lingered on this side. He saw the visible, recognized the visible, and found his place in this universe. He now no longer sought the reality, and his goal was now dwelt on neither side of the visible.

How beautiful the universe was when one just looked at it, just looked at it with the intention of searching for none, just looked at it with a simple gaze and just looked at it with a childlike wonder. How beautiful the moon and the stars were. How beautiful the brook, the shore, the forest, the rock, the goat, the golden beetle, the flower, and the butterfly were. How beautiful and how pleasant it was to go through the universe with an awakened mind, with a childlike heart, with an immediate concern, and with trust.

Elsewhere, the sun burned fiercely. Elsewhere, there was cool in the forest shade. Elsewhere, there were pumpkins and bananas. The days and the nights were short. Every hour passed quickly like a sail on the sea, and beneath the sail was a ship full of treasures and full of joy.

Siddhartha saw a group of monkeys swinging on high branches in the depths of the forest and heard them crying wildly and eagerly. Siddhartha saw a ram following a sheep to mate. In a lake of rushes, Siddhartha saw a starving pike making the chase in evening hunger. While fluttering around, swarms of glistening young fish moved anxiously away from it. Strength and desire were reflected in the swiftly moving whirls of water formed by the raging pursuer.

All these had always been here, but Siddhartha never once noticed them. He lived as if he was never present.

Now that he was present, so he belonged to this universe. Through his eyes, he saw light and shadows. Through his mind, he was aware of the moon and stars.

On the way, Siddhartha recalled everything that he experienced in the garden of Jetavana—the teachings that he heard from the holy Buddha, the farewell that he bade to Govinda, and the conversation that he had with the Illustrious One. He recollected each word that he talked to the Illustrious One, and he was astonished that he said things, which he, himself, did not even really know back then.

What Siddhartha told the Buddha at that time—that the Buddha's enlightenment was not teachable and that Buddha's wisdom and secret were inexpressible and incommunicable—and which Siddhartha experienced at that enlightened hour were just what he now set off to experience and just what he now began to experience. Siddhartha had to gain experience himself.

Siddhartha had known for a long time that his *Self* was Atman, which had the same eternal origin with Brahman—known as the *Great Self*, but he had never once found his *Self*. Why had he never once found his *Self*? Was it perhaps because he had always trapped it in the net of thoughts?

The body was, of course, certainly not the *Self*. Feelings, thoughts, understanding, judiciousness, acquired wisdom to draw conclusions, and acquired art to spin off new thoughts from existing thoughts were not the *Self*, either. No, this world of thoughts was still on this side of the visible; hence, it led to no goal if one attempted to destroy his six roots of sensations in order to nourish the *Self* with thoughts and erudition.

Both thoughts and senses were fine things because behind both of them lay hidden the ultimate meaning. It was worthwhile to listen to them both and to play with them both—neither to despise nor to overrate either one of them but to listen intently to both of them instead. Siddhartha would only strive after whatever the inward voice commanded him. He would never tarry anywhere except for where the voice advised him.

Why did Gotama once sit down beneath the Bodhi tree in his greatest hour after he attained enlightenment? He heard a voice. A voice in his own heart commanded him to seek rest under the Bodhi tree. He took no recourse to mortification of the flesh, offered no sacrifice to the gods, performed no bath at the holy ablutions, and prayed to no one. Without eating, drinking, sleeping, and dreaming, he only listened to the voice in his heart. He only complied with his inward voice and obeyed to no other external command. This was good, and this was essential. Nothing else was necessary to him.

During the night, as Siddhartha slept in a ferryman's straw hut, he had a dream. He dreamt that Govinda stood before him, in the yellow robe of the ascetic. Govinda looked sad and asked him, "Why did you leave me?" Thereupon, Siddhartha embraced Govinda and wrapped his arms around his friend's chest. As he drew Govinda closer to his breast and wanted to kiss his friend, his friend was no longer Govinda but a woman. And out of the woman's gown emerged a full breast, and Siddhartha lay there and drank. How sweet and how strong the taste of the milk from the breast was! It was the taste of the woman and the man, was the taste of the sun and the moon, was the taste of the forest and the mountain, was the taste of the animal and the flower, was the taste of the fruit and the seed, and was the taste of the desire and the pleasure. How intoxicating the taste of the milk was!

When Siddhartha woke up, the pale river was shimmering past the door of the hut, and the cry of an owl was reverberating from the deep forest. The howling sounds of the owl were deep and clear.

As the day began, Siddhartha asked his host, the ferryman, to take him across the river. The ferryman took Siddhartha across on his bamboo raft. The broad sheet of water shimmered pink in the light of the morning.

"This river is beautiful," said Siddhartha to his companion.

"Yes," replied the ferryman, "it is a beautiful river. I love it above everything else. I have often listened to it, have usually gazed at it, and have always learned something from it. One can learn much from a river."

"Thank you, good man," said Siddhartha as he landed on the other side. "I am afraid that I have no gift to give you and have no money to pay you. I am a homeless person, a Brahmin's son, and a Samana."

"Yes, I could see that," said the ferryman with a smile, "and I do not expect any gift or any form of payment from you. You will give it to me some other time."

"Do you think so?" asked Siddhartha merrily.

"Certainly," replied the ferryman cheerfully, "I have learned this from the river. Everything comes back, and so do you, the Samana. You will come back. Now farewell, may your friendship be my payment! May you think of me when you offer sacrifices to the gods!"

While smiling, they parted from each other.

Siddhartha was pleased with the ferryman's friendliness.

"He is like Govinda," Siddhartha mumbled and smiled. "All people I met on the way are like Govinda. They all are grateful even though they, themselves, deserve thanks. They all are subservient even though they do not have to be. They all wish to be my friends, wish to obey me, and wish to think very little. People are like children."

At midday, Siddhartha passed through a village. Children danced here and there in the lane in front of the clay huts. They played with pumpkin-stones and mussels. They shouted and wrestled with each other, but in a hurry, they timidly ran away when the strange Samana appeared.

At the end of the village, the path ran alongside a brook, and at the edge of the brook, a young woman was kneeling and washing clothes. When Siddhartha greeted her, she raised her head and looked up at him with a smile so that he could see the sparkling whites of her eyes shining. He called out a benediction to her as if it was a custom among the travelers and asked how far the road still was from the large town.

Thereupon, she stood up and came towards Siddhartha while her moist lips attractively gleamed in her young face. She exchanged light remarks with him and asked him if he had already eaten or not yet. She also asked him if it was true that the Samanas slept alone in the forest at night and could not have any woman with them.

She then placed her left foot onto Siddhartha's right foot and made a gesture which a woman made when she invited a man to enjoy the pleasure of love—the kind of love enjoyment that the holy books called "ascending the tree". Siddhartha felt his blood kindled right at this very moment. And as soon as he recognized his dream from the night before, he stooped towards the woman a little and kissed the brown tip of her breast. He then looked up and saw a lustful desire on her smiling face and a pleading longing in her half-closed eyes.

Siddhartha, himself, also felt a longing and sensed a stir of sex within him. Even though his hands were more than ready to seize her, he hesitated for a moment because he had never touched a woman before. Right at this instant, he suddenly heard his inward voice, and the voice said "No!"

Immediately, all enchantments disappeared from the young woman's smiling face, but Siddhartha saw nothing but the ardent glance of a passionate young woman. Gently, he stroked her cheek and quickly disappeared from the disappointed woman into the bamboo wood.

Before the evening of that day, he reached a large town, and he was very glad because he had a desire to be with people. He had lived in the woods for a long time; hence, the ferryman's straw hut in which he slept the night before was the first roof he had over his head for a long time.

Just right outside of the town, near a beautiful unfenced grove, the wanderer met a small train of menservants and maidservants carrying loaded baskets. In the middle of the train, inside an ornamented sedan chair carried by four people was a woman, the mistress, sitting on red cushions beneath a colored awning.

Siddhartha stood still at the entrance to the grove and watched the procession of the menservants and the maidservants carrying loaded baskets. He looked at the sedan chair and the woman in it. Beneath heaped-up black hair, he saw a very bright, very sweet, and very clever face, which was livened up by a bright red mouth like a freshly cut fig, a pair of artful eyebrows painted in a high arch, a pair of lustrous dark observant eyes, and a clear slender neck above the greenish gold gown. The woman's hands were firm and smooth, but they were long and slender. Broad gold bangles in matte and shine finish on her wrists brought out her beauty even more.

Siddhartha saw how beautiful she was, and his heart rejoiced. He bowed low as the sedan chair passed close by him, but he then raised himself again to gaze at her bright, fair, and lovely face. At that moment, he let himself sink deeper into her clever arched eyes for a while and inhaled the fragrance of a perfume, which he could not recognize what the smell was. For a moment, the beautiful women nodded and smiled with him, but she then disappeared into the grove, followed by the servants.

"And so," murmured Siddhartha, "I enter this town under a lucky star." He felt the urge to enter the grove immediately, but he thought it over and decided not to go in because it just occurred to him how the menservants and the maidservants looked at him at the entrance. Their fleeting glances were so scornful, so distrustful, and so dismissing.

"I am still a Samana," spoke Siddhartha softly to himself, "still an ascetic, and still a beggar. I cannot remain to be any of them. I cannot enter the grove like whomever that I resemble the most right now."

He then laughed it off.

On the way to the town, whenever Siddhartha came across people, he inquired about the grove and the name of the woman. He eventually learned that it was the grove of Kamala, the well-known courtesan. He also learned that besides the grove, she also owned a house in the town.

Siddhartha then entered the town with a goal in mind. He now had a goal, the only one. To pursue this goal, he quickened his pace to survey the town, wandered through the maze of streets, stood still in many places, and rested on stone steps along the river.

In the evening on the same day, Siddhartha made friends with a barber's assistant whom Siddhartha first saw him working in the shade of an arch. Siddhartha again saw him praying in the Vishnu temple where he later shared with Siddhartha the story about how Lord Vishnu married to Goddess Lakshmi.

Lord Vishnu married to Goddess Lakshmi

During the night, Siddhartha slept in one of the boats that were anchored on the river. Early in the morning on the next day, before the first customer arrived at the barbershop, Siddhartha asked the barber's assistant to help him shave off his beard, comb his hair, and rub it with fine oil. He then went to bathe in the river.

In the late afternoon, when the beautiful Kamala was approaching her grove in the ornamented sedan chair, Siddhartha had already been waiting for her at the entrance. He bowed to her and received her greeting in return. He then beckoned to the manservant who was the last one in the procession and asked the manservant to announce to his mistress that a young Brahmin desired to speak to her. After a little while, the manservant returned and asked Siddhartha to follow him. He silently conducted Siddhartha into a pavilion where Kamala lay on a couch and left Siddhartha there with her.

"Did you not stand outside the entrance yesterday and greet me?" asked Kamala.

"Yes indeed. I saw you yesterday and greeted you," said Siddhartha with a nod.

"But did you not have a beard and long hair that were covered with dust yesterday?" continued Kamala.

"You observed very well, and you saw everything," said Siddhartha with a smile, "You saw Siddhartha, the Brahmin's son, who left his parents' home in order to become a Samana in the forest and was a Samana for three years. Now, however, Siddhartha has left the forest in order to go on his own way, and the Samana has left the ascetic life in order to gain a real-life experience himself. When I headed towards this town, the first person I met before I reached the town was you. Today, I have come here to tell you, O Kamala, that you are the first woman to whom Siddhartha has spoken without lowering his eyes. Never again shall I lower my eyes when I meet a beautiful woman."

Kamala smiled while playing with her fan made of peacock feathers and asked, "Is it all that Siddhartha has come here today to tell me?"

"Yes, I have come today to tell you all that and to thank you because you are so beautiful. And if it does not displease you, Kamala, I would like to ask you to be my friend and also to be my teacher because I do not know any secret of the art of which you are the mistress."

Thereupon, Kamala laughed aloud, "It has never been my experience to receive a Samana who comes from the wood and desires to learn from me. Never has a Samana with long hair and an old, torn loincloth come to me. Many young men, including Brahmins' sons, come to me, but they all come to me in fine clothes and in fine shoes. They all have perfume in their hair and money in their purses. That is how these young men come to me, O Samana."

Siddhartha said, "I am already beginning to learn from you. I already learned something yesterday. Already, I have gotten rid of my beard. Already, I have combed and oiled my hair. O my most beautiful woman, there is not much more that I am lacking—only fine clothes, fine shoes, and money in my purse. Siddhartha undertook many challenges that are much more difficult than those trivial things and attained them all. How could I not attain what I have decided to undertake yesterday—to be your friend and to learn the pleasures of love from you? You will find me an apt pupil, Kamala. I have learned a lot more difficult things than what you are going to teach me. So, Siddhartha, as he is, with oil in his hair, with no fine clothes, with no shoes, and with no money is not good enough for you, is he?"

Kamala laughed and shook her head, "No, he is not yet good enough. He must have clothes, fine clothes; he must have shoes, fine shoes; he must have money, plenty of money; and he must have presents, expensive presents for Kamala. Do you know now, the Samana from the wood? Do you understand?"

"I understand very well," uttered Siddhartha aloud in good spirits. "How could I fail to understand when words like those come from such a lovely mouth? Your mouth is like a freshly cut fig, O Kamala. My lips are also red and fresh, and they will fit yours well. You will see. But tell me, my beautiful Kamala, are you not at all afraid of this strange Samana from the forest? Are you not at all afraid of the Samana who wants to learn about love from you for the first time?"

Kamala smiled and said with full confidence, "Why should I be afraid of a Samana from the forest?"

Kamala reiterated with a broad grin and a charming frown on her face, "Afraid of a stupid Samana who comes from the jackals and does not know anything about women?"

Siddhartha felt a jolt of pleasure, "Oh, this Samana is strong, and he is not afraid of anything. He could force you, O my beautiful maiden. He could rob you, and he could even hurt you."

"No, the Samana, I am not afraid at all," Kamala giggled and shook her head. "Has a Samana or a Brahmin ever feared that someone could come and strike him, ever feared that someone could come and rob him of his knowledge, ever feared that someone could come and steal his piety, and ever feared that someone could come and take his power to derive profound thoughts away from him? The answer is 'No, never' because they all belong to him. He can give them of in whichever way he wants and to whomever he wishes—only if he wishes. That is exactly how it is with Kamala and with the pleasures of love. Fair and red are Kamala's lips; however, if you try to kiss them against Kamala's will, not one drop of sweetness will you obtain from them even though they know very well how to give sweetness! You are an apt pupil, Siddhartha, so you may also wish to learn this as well, 'One can beg for love, can buy love with money, can be presented with love, and can even find love in the streets, but one can never steal love. You have misunderstood, the Samana. Yes, it would be a pity if a fine young man like you misunderstood this whole notion."

Siddhartha bowed and smiled, "You are right, Kamala. It would be a pity.

It would be a great pity. It would be a very great pity if Siddhartha misunderstood this whole notion. No, no drop of sweetness should be lost from your lips or from mine. Therefore, Siddhartha will come again when he has what he is lacking in—fine clothes, fine shoes, and a lot of money. But tell me, fair Kamala, can you not give me a piece of advice?"

"Advice?" smiled Kamala fondly, "Why not? Who would not willingly give advice to a poor, ignorant Samana who comes from the jackals in the forest?"

"Dear Kamala, where can I go in order to obtain those three things as quickly as possible?"

"O my dear friend," laughed Kamala, "many people want to know the answer to the question that you just asked me. You must take advantage of what you have learned in order to earn money, to buy clothes, and to obtain shoes. There is no other way for a poor man to earn money unless he knows something or he is capable of doing something, otherwise."

"I can think; I can wait; and I can fast," replied Siddhartha quickly.

"Nothing else?" said Kamala indifferently.

"Nothing else really," Siddhartha remained silent for a little while, but all of a sudden, he uttered, "O yes, I can also compose poetry. Will you give me a kiss for a poem?"

"I will do so if your poem pleases me," replied Kamala affectionately with a smile, "What is it called?"

After thinking for a moment, Siddhartha recited this verse,

> "Into her grove went the fair Kamala.
> At the entrance to the grove stood the brown Samana.
> As he saw the Lotus flower,
> Deeply, he bowed.
> Smiling, acknowledged Kamala.
> Better, thought the young Samana,
> To make sacrifices to the fair Kamala
> Than to offer sacrifices to the gods."

Kamala clapped her hands loudly and repeatedly to show how surprised and how pleased she was with the clever contents of the poem. She continued clapping so long that the golden bangles tinkled.

"Your poetry is very good, brown Samana, and truly, there is nothing to lose if I give you a kiss for it," smiled Kamala.

She drew him to her with her alluring eyes. He put his face against hers and placed his lips against her lips, which were like a freshly cut fig. Kamala kissed him deeply, and to Siddhartha's great astonishment, he felt how much she taught him, how clever she was, how skillfully she mastered him, how appealingly she repulsed him, and how attractive she lured him. After this first long kiss, he felt how delighted he was to pine for a long series of many other kisses, all different, awaiting him.

Siddhartha stood still while breathing deeply. At that very moment, he was like a child who was completely astonished at the fullness of knowledge and at the experience that unfolded itself before his eyes.

"Your poetry is, in fact, very good," said Kamala, "if I were rich, I would give you money for it. However, with poetry alone, it will be very hard for you to earn as much money as you want because you will need a lot. If you want to be Kamala's friend, you will need a lot of money."

"How wonderfully you can kiss, Kamala!" stammered Siddhartha.

"Yes, indeed," replied Kamala without hesitating, "that is why I am not lacking in clothes, in shoes, in bangles, and in all sorts of pretty things. But now what are you going to do?"

"Can you do anything else besides thinking, waiting, fasting, and composing poetry?" asked Kamala in a sarcastic and condescending tone of voice to provoke the naive Samana.

"Oh, there are a few more. I know how to sing sacrificial songs," said Siddhartha cheerfully, "but I will not sing them anymore. I know how to recite incantations, but I will not recite them anymore, either. I also read the scriptures and write—"

"Wait," interrupted Kamala abruptly, "you can read and write?"

"Certainly I can. Many people can do that," said Siddhartha calmly.

"No, it is not many people. Most people cannot. I, for example, can neither read nor write. Very good, it is very good that you know how to read and write. You might even need the incantations."

But right at that moment, a manservant entered and whispered something in his mistress's ear.

"I have a visitor," said Kamala, "hurry and disappear, Siddhartha, nobody must see you here. I will see you again tomorrow."

However, she ordered a maidservant to give the holy Brahmin a white gown. Without quite knowing what was happening, Siddhartha was conducted away by the manservant, through a circuitous route to a garden house where he was presented with the white gown. The manservant then guided Siddhartha to the thicket and carefully instructed him to leave the grove without being seen by anyone as quickly as possible.

Contentedly, Siddhartha did what he was told. By being accustomed to the forest, he silently made his way out of the grove and over the hedge. Cheerfully, he returned to the town with the rolled-up white gown under his arm.

Siddhartha stood at the door of an inn where travelers stayed. In silence, he begged for food, and in quiet, he accepted a piece of rice cake. He thought for a second and then mumbled, "Perhaps tomorrow, I will no longer need to beg for food."

Suddenly, Siddhartha was overwhelmed with a feeling of pride and asserted himself, "Siddhartha is no longer a Samana, so it no longer fits that he should beg for food."

Siddhartha then gave the rice cake to a dog and remained without food for the rest of the day.

"How simple life is in this town," rationalized Siddhartha. "It has no difficulty at all. Everything was difficult, irksome, and finally hopeless when I was a Samana. Now, everything is easy. It is as easy as the kissing instruction that Kamala gives. I only need clothes, shoes, and money, and that is all. They are easy goals which do not disturb one's sleep."

Since Siddhartha had inquired about Kamala's town house a long while back, he went there on the next day to visit her.

"Things are going well," Kamala called across to Siddhartha. "Kamaswami invites you to come and see him. He expects to see you at his house. He is the richest merchant in this town. If you please him, he will take you into his service. Be clever, brown Samana! I had other people mentioned your name to him. Be friendly towards him because he is very powerful. However, I do not want you to be too modest before him since I do not want you to be his servant. I want you to be his equal; otherwise, I shall not be pleased with you. Kamaswami is beginning to grow old and indolent. If you please him, he will place great confidence in you."

Siddhartha thanked Kamala and laughed. Soon after she learned that he had not eaten anything that day and the day before, she ordered the servants to bring bread and fruit to him. She then served him herself.

"You have been lucky," she told him when he was ready to take leave of her, "One door after the other is being opened to you. How does that come about? You do have a charm, do you not?"

Siddhartha said, "Yesterday, I told you that I knew how to think, how to wait, and how to fast, but you did not consider them to be useful. Before long, you will see that they are very useful, Kamala. You will see that stupid Samanas in the forest learn and know many useful things, which are of great value. The day before yesterday, I was still an unkempt beggar. Yesterday, I already kissed Kamala. Soon, I will be a merchant, will have money, and will have all those things, which you value."

"Quite," agreed Kamala, "but what would you have had if you had not met me? How would you have connected with Kamaswami if I had not had your name mentioned to him? How would you have proceeded if I had not given you advice? What would you have done if Kamala had not helped you?"

"My dear Kamala," said Siddhartha, "when I came to you in your grove, I made the first step. It was my intention to learn about love from the most beautiful woman. From the moment I made that resolution, I knew that I would execute it and would succeed. I also knew that you would help me. I knew it from the first glance you gave me at the entrance to the grove."

"What if I did not want to—" argued Kamala with a bashful charm.

"But you already did want to," Siddhartha quickly interrupted Kamala before she even had a chance to finish the sentence. "Listen, my dear Kamala, when you throw a stone into the water, it finds the quickest way to reach the bottom of the water. It is the same when Siddhartha has an aim, a goal. He does nothing. He waits; he thinks; and he fasts, but he goes through the affairs of the world as fast as the stone goes through the water. Like the stone which does not do anything, Siddhartha will not do anything and will not let himself bestir. He will not allow anything that opposes his goal to enter his mind. He will let his goal draw himself and will let himself experience the free falling feeling. This practice is one among many that Siddhartha learned from the Samanas in the woods. It is what fools call magic, and it is what fools are deceived into thinking that demons actually perform. Nothing is performed by demons, and there is no demon. Everyone can perform magic. Everyone can reach his goal if he can think, can wait, and can fast."

Kamala was fascinated by how Siddhartha talked and listened to him with full concentration. She loved his voice and loved the look in his eyes.

"Perhaps, it is as you say, my friend," spoke Kamala softly, "but perhaps, it is also because Siddhartha is a handsome young man and because Siddhartha's glance pleases women. This perhaps explains why he is lucky."

Siddhartha kissed Kamala and said goodbye. "May it be so, my teacher! May my glance always please you! May good fortune always come to me from you!"

Remark: Siddhartha recalled what he told the Buddha—the Buddha's enlightenment was not teachable and that Buddha's wisdom and secret were inexpressible and incommunicable—and recalled which he experienced at that enlightened hour. He insisted that he had to experience his own enlightenment.

On the way to town, he convinced himself that this world of thoughts was still on this side of the visible; hence, it led to no goal if one attempted to destroy his six roots of sensations in order to nourish the *Self* with thoughts and erudition. With this line of reasoning, he allowed his six roots of sensations to take a free rein to passions and forgot all about his previous beliefs—happiness and beauty were all illusions of six roots of sensations. All were doomed to decay. The world tasted bitter. Life was a pain. Kamala was his first test . .

CHAPTER 6

AMONGST THE PEOPLE

Siddhartha went to see Kamaswami, the merchant, and he was shown to go into a rich house. Servants conducted him across costly carpets to a large room where he waited for the master of the house.

Kamaswami entered the room. He was a supple, lively man with gray hair. Through the sharp-wittedness in his eyes and the prudence in his sight, everyone could tell that he was a clever individual with a sensual mouth. The master and the visitor greeted each other in a friendly manner.

"I have been told," began the merchant, "that you are a Brahmin, a learned man, but you now wish to seek service with a merchant. Then, are you, Brahmin, so in need that you must seek service?"

"No," replied Siddhartha, "I am not even in need, and I, in fact, have never once been in need. I came from the Samanas with whom I lived for a long time."

The merchant argued, "If you came from the Samanas, how could it be that you are not in need? Are all the Samanas completely without possessions?"

"I possess nothing," said Siddhartha, "if that is what you mean. Of course, I am certainly without possessions. I own nothing, but I surrender everything of my own free will and live under no duress. Hence, I am not in need."

The merchant attempted to establish the case, "But how will you live if you are without possessions?"

"I have never thought about it, Sir," said Siddhartha calmly, "I have been without possessions for nearly three years, and I have never once thought about how I could survive."

"So you have lived on the possessions of others?" the merchant challenged.

"Apparently, it appears to be that way," smiled Siddhartha, "but the merchant also lives on the possessions of others."

"Well spoken, my friend," the merchant was surprised by Siddhartha's words, "but the merchant does not take from others for nothing. He gives his goods in exchange."

"That seems to be the way things work in life," concluded Siddhartha, "Everyone takes, and everyone gives. Life is like that, I assume."

"Ah," the merchant refused to give up, "but if you are without possessions, how can you give?"

"Everyone gives what he has," explained Siddhartha patiently, "The soldier gives strength; the merchant gives goods; the teacher gives instruction; the farmer gives rice crop; and the fisherman gives fish."

The merchant continued to challenge, "Very well. So what can you give? What can you give from what you have learned?"

"I can think; I can wait; and I can fast," replied Siddhartha proudly.

The merchant's jaw dropped, "Is that all?"

"I think that is all," smiled Siddhartha.

The merchant asked as a slight frown creased his forehead, "And of what use are they? Fasting, for example, what good is that?"

"It is of great value, Sir," explained Siddhartha proudly, "If a man has nothing to eat, fasting is then the most intelligent thing he can do. If, for instance, Siddhartha had not learned how to fast, he would have had to seek some kind of work today, regardless of whether with you or with someone else, for hunger would have driven him. But as it is, Siddhartha can wait calmly. He is neither in a hurry nor impatient because he is not in need. He can ward off hunger for a long time, and he can laugh with it. Therefore, fasting is useful, Sir."

"You are right, Samana," the merchant repeatedly nodded his head and put his index finger to his lips to signal the Samana to silence, "Wait for a moment."

Kamaswami went out and returned with a roll of paper. He handed it to his guest and inquired, "Can you read this?"

Siddhartha looked at the roll of paper on which a sale agreement was written, and he began to read the contents.

"Excellent," said Kamaswami.

He then gave Siddhartha a sheet of paper and a pen and said, "Can you write something on this paper for me?"

Siddhartha wrote something on the paper and returned it to Kamaswami.

Kamaswami read what Siddhartha wrote aloud, "Writing is good, but thinking is better. Cleverness is good, but patience is better."

The merchant praised Siddhartha, "You write very well. We shall still have plenty to discuss, but today, I invite you to be my guest and welcome you to live in my house."

Siddhartha thanked him and accepted the invitation. He now lived in the merchant's house. One servant brought Siddhartha clothes and shoes while another servant prepared a bath for him. Everything was prepared for him on a daily basis. Splendid meals were served twice a day, but Siddhartha only ate once a day and neither ate meat nor drank wine.

Kamaswami talked to Siddhartha about his business, showed Siddhartha the goods, led Siddhartha to his warehouses, and went over his accounts with Siddhartha.

Siddhartha learned many new things, but he heard much and said very little. As things unfolded at the Kamaswami's house, Siddhartha remembered Kamala's words. He was never servile to the merchant, but on the contrary, he compelled the merchant to treat him as an equal and, sometimes, even more than an equal.

Kamaswami conducted his business with great care and with great passion, but Siddhartha regarded it all as a game with rules. Since Siddhartha endeavored to learn the rules well, none of the business matters stirred his heart.

Siddhartha had not been in Kamaswami's house for long, but he already took the better part of Kamaswami's business. Daily, however, at the hour the beautiful Kamala invited him, he visited her in handsome clothes, in fine shoes, and with her favorite presents. He learned many things from her wise red lips. Her smooth, gentle hands taught him many things.

Siddhartha, who was still a boy as regards love and was inclined to plunge into the depths of it blindly and insatiably, was taught by Kamala that one could not have pleasure without granting pleasure in return. She taught him that every gesture, every caress, every touch, every glance, and every single part of the body had its own secret. Only those who knew these secrets could enjoy the pleasures, and only those who understood these secrets could give the pleasures. She also taught him that lovers were not supposed to separate from each other after making love without admiring each other, without being conquered by the other, and without conquering the other. Her enlightenment was to prevent neither the feeling of satiation nor the feeling of desolation from arising and to prevent no one from having the horrid feeling of taking advantage of the other or of being taken advantage by the other. After spending many wonderful hours with the clever, beautiful courtesan, Siddhartha eventually became her pupil, became her lover, and became her dear friend. The value and the meaning of his present life, indeed, lay here with Kamala, not with Kamaswami's business.

Not only did Kamaswami entrust Siddhartha with the writing of important letters and orders, but he also grew accustomed to conferring with Siddhartha about important affairs. Before long, he realized that Siddhartha understood very little about rice, wool, shipping, and trading, but he also realized that Siddhartha had a happy knack and had a natural instinct. With this natural instinct, he became well conscious that Siddhartha surpassed him in calmness, in equanimity, in the art of listening, and in the skill of making a good impression on strange people.

"This Brahmin," Kamaswami talked to a friend of his, "is no real merchant and will never be one. He has never once been absorbed in the business, but he does have the secret of those people to whom success readily comes by itself. I do not know whatever it is—whether he was born under a lucky star or whether it is magic or whether he has learned the secret from the Samanas, but he always seems to be playing at business. Business has never made a great impression on him and has never once mastered him. Evidently, he never fears of failure and never once worries over a potential loss."

The friend then advised the merchant, "Give him only a third of the profits of the business, which he conducts for you, but make him share the same proportion of losses when there is one. This lopsided package deal will motivate him to become more enthusiastic."

Kamaswami followed his friend's advice, but Siddhartha had very little concern about it.

If there was a profit, Siddhartha accepted it calmly. If there was a loss, he laughed and said, "Oh well, this transaction went badly!" Siddhartha, in fact, did seem indifferent towards all business matters.

One day, Siddhartha travelled to a village in order to buy a large rice harvest. But when he arrived there, the rice was already sold to another merchant. Instead of being disappointed and going home, Siddhartha decided to remain in the village for several days. He entertained the farmers, gave money to the children, attended a wedding, and finally returned from the journey feeling completely satisfied.

After coming back from the trip, Kamaswami reproached Siddhartha for not returning immediately and for wasting time as well as money.

"Do not scold, my dear friend," replied Siddhartha. "Nothing has ever been achieved by scolding. If a loss has been sustained, I will bear all the cost because I am very satisfied with this journey. I have become acquainted with many people, and I have made a good friend with a Brahmin. Children sat on my knee; farmers showed me their fields; and nobody took me for a merchant."

"All things have been fine," admitted Kamaswami reluctantly, "but you are, in reality, a merchant. Why did you travel to the village in the first place? Did you travel for your pleasure?"

"Certainly, I travelled for my pleasure," laughed Siddhartha, "Why not? I have become acquainted with many people and with many new districts. I have enjoyed good friendships and have earned trust from the villagers. If I were Kamaswami, I would depart immediately and would feel very annoyed when I learned that I was unable to make a purchase. Besides, I would be very, very distressed for I realized that I lost so much time and money. Unlike Kamaswami, I spent a number of good days there, learned many new things, enjoyed much pleasure, and hurt neither others nor myself with annoyance or hastiness. If I ever go there again, perhaps to buy a later harvest or to accomplish other purposes, friendly people will receive me, and I will be glad that I had not previously displayed any hastiness or displeasure. Regardless of whatever the case may be, let it rest, my friend, and do not hurt yourself by scolding. If it came to the day when you believed that this Siddhartha brought harm to you and that you were not pleased with Siddhartha, you would just say one word, and Siddhartha would go on his way. Until then, however, let us be good friends."

The merchant made a great attempt to convince Siddhartha that Siddhartha was eating his, Kamaswami's, bread, but his effort was in vain. Siddhartha actually ate his own bread. To be more precise, they both ate the bread of others, the bread of everybody.

Siddhartha was never concerned about Kamaswami's troubles, and Kamaswami always had many troubles. When a transaction seemed to be on the verge of failing, when a consignment of goods was lost, and when a debtor refused to pay, Kamaswami was never capable of resolving anything on his own. He could never once persuade his colleagues to believe that it served no purpose to utter troubled words, to boil over with anger, to fly into a passion, to form wrinkles on the forehead, and to toss and turn all night long.

One time, when Kamaswami reminded Siddhartha that Siddhartha had learned everything from him, Siddhartha calmly replied with a satirical smile, "Do not make such jokes, my friend. I have learned from you how much a basket of fish costs, and how much interest one can claim for lending money. These are your knowledge, my friend. Let us get one thing straight. I did not learn from you how to think, my dear Kamaswami. I do believe, however, that it would be better if you learned from me how to think instead."

Indeed, Siddhartha's heart was not in business. To him, business was simply useful because it brought him money, which he needed to present to Kamala as presents. In reality, it brought him a lot more money than he really needed. Moreover, Siddhartha's sympathy and curiosity lay only with people whose work, whose troubles, whose pleasures, and whose follies were more unknown to him and were more remote from him than the moon ever was.

Although he found it so easy to speak to everyone, to live with everyone, and to learn from everyone, he was very conscious of the fact that there was something, which separated him from everyone. Perhaps, the thing that made him different from the rest of the others lay in the fact that he was once a Samana. He saw how people lived and how people acted. They lived as if they were like children, and they acted as if they were like animals. In spite of everything, he loved them for who they were, but at the same time, he despised them for how they acted.

He saw them toiling, saw them suffering, and saw them turning gray over things that, to him, did not seem worth the price. Money, transitory power, passing indulgences, and fleeting sensual pleasures all were trivial and illusory to him. He saw them scolding each other, hitting each other, injuring each other, and even destroying each other. Most ironically, he saw them lamenting over pain that the Samanas would just laugh and saw them suffering from deprivation that the Samanas would never feel.

Siddhartha accepted everything that people brought to him. The merchant who brought him linen for sale was welcome. The debtor who sought a loan was welcome in the same way. The beggar who beseeched food and money was also received equally. Sometimes, a few beggars stayed for hours to tell him stories of their poverty even though none of them was nearly as poor as any Samana. He did not treat the rich foreign merchants who came from afar any differently from poor servants who gave him a shave. The peddlers, whom he let himself be robbed of a few small coins when he bought their bananas, also received the same kind of treatment.

When Kamaswami came to Siddhartha to tell him about his worries or came to Siddhartha to reproach him for creating unfavorable transactions, Siddhartha listened to him curiously and attentively, but at the same time, Siddhartha was amazed at his worries and reproaches. Siddhartha tried to understand him and tried to concede to him a little where it seemed necessary. However, when needed, Siddhartha turned away from him and focused his attention on the next person who needed Siddhartha more.

Many people came to Siddhartha, but they all came to him for different reasons. Many came to trade with him; many came to deceive him; many came to listen to him; many came to elicit his sympathy; and many came to ask for his advice. He offered a good deal; he let himself be cheated a little; he provided suggestion; he sympathized; and he gave advice. All these games and these passions, which people were playing with him, had occupied his mind as much as the gods and the Brahmins occupied his psyche in the past.

At times, Siddhartha heard within him a soft, gentle voice, which quietly reminded him and quietly complained to him. The voice was so calm and so faint that he could hardly hear it. He then suddenly realized clearly that he was leading a strange life, that he was doing many foolish things, that he was playing a passing game, that he was enjoying happiness's, and that he was taking pleasure in satisfaction, but the real life, itself, was flowing past him without even touching him.

Like a player who played with his ball, Siddhartha played with his business, had fun with the people around him, enjoyed watching them lead their childish lives, and derived amusement for him from their animal-like acts, but his heart and his real nature were neither in business nor with the people. His real *Self* had aimlessly wandered elsewhere far away, had invisibly roved from place to place, and had no longer involved in his present life. Sometimes, he was afraid of the way he thought about his life and wished that he could share their daily childish affairs with intensity and could take part in life with his heart and his real nature. He would much rather to participate, to enjoy, and to live his life as if they lived theirs than to only be on the sideline as an onlooker.

Siddhartha regularly visited the beautiful Kamala and passionately learned the art of love in which, more than all other things, giving and taking became one. He talked to her, learned from her, gave her advice, and received her advice. She understood him better than Govinda had once understood him, and she bore a resemblance to Siddhartha much more closely than Govinda ever resembled him in the past.

One day, Siddhartha told Kamala, "You are like me. You are different from other people. You are Kamala and no one else. Within you, there has always been a sanctuary or stillness where you can come for a retreat whenever you wish or where you can come to be your own *Self* whenever you desire, just as I can. Very few people have this capacity even though everyone could have it."

"Not all people are clever," said Kamala.

"It has nothing to do with cleverness, Kamala," said Siddhartha, "Kamaswami is just as clever as I am, but he has no sanctuary. Many other people have a sanctuary within them, but they are like children when it comes to understanding. Most people, Kamala, are like falling leaves which keep drifting along with the tumbling tumbleweeds, keep fluttering in the wind, and keep turning around and around in the air until they completely fall down on the ground. On the contrary, among many who have a sanctuary within them, a few are like stars, which keep travelling on a defined path. No wind can exert any influence on them. It seems as if they carry an inner magnetic compass that keep them staying on their defined path. Among all the wise men that I have known, there is one person who is perfect in this respect. I can never forget him. He is Gotama, the Illustrious One, who preaches the gospel. Thousands and thousands of young men listen to his teachings every day, and thousands of young monks follow his instructions every hour, but they all are falling leaves. They have no wisdom and have no guide within themselves."

Kamala looked at Siddhartha and smiled. "You are talking about him again, my dear," she said, "Also, you have Samana thoughts again."

Siddhartha was silent, and they played the game of love, one of the thirty or forty different games, which Kamala knew. Her body was as supple as that of a jaguar and as lithe as that of a sharpshooter's bow. Those who learned about love from her also learned many pleasures and many secrets.

Kamala played with Siddhartha for a long time. She repulsed him, overwhelmed him, conquered him, and rejoiced at her mastery. She kept playing with him until he was completely overcome and was exhausted lying by her side.

The courtesan bent over Siddhartha. She looked long at his face and deep into his eyes that were grown tired. Thoughtfully, she said, "You are the best lover that I have ever had. You are stronger, suppler, and more willing than most others are. You have learned my art well, Siddhartha. Some day, when I am older, I want to bear your child. Yet, my dear, you have remained a Samana all this time. You do not really love me. You love nobody. Is that not true, my dear?"

"Maybe," said Siddhartha wearily. "I am like you. You cannot love anyone either; otherwise, how could you practice love as an art? Perhaps, those who like us cannot love. Only can the ordinary people, and that is their secret.

Remark: Siddhartha continued to experience other tests in the material life through Kamaswami, trading business, the life of the rich, the childlike people, the peddlers, the beggars, the debtors . . .

CHAPTER 7

SAMSARA

For a long time, Siddhartha had lived in the material world, but he actually did not belong to it. The six roots of sensations that he had deadened during his ardent Samana years were again awakened. He had tasted riches, passion, and power, but for a long time, he remained a Samana in his heart. Clever Kamala had long recognized this. His life was always directed by the art of thinking, waiting, and fasting. The people in this material world, the ordinary people, were still alien to him, just as much as he was apart from them.

The years passed by, but Siddhartha hardly bothered to notice their passing. Because of being enveloped by comfortable circumstances, he had become rich. Not long after working with Kamaswami, he had possessed a house of his own, the servants of his own, and a garden of his own on the outskirts of the town by the river. People liked him. They came to him whenever they wanted money or needed advice. However, besides Kamala, he had no close friend.

The glorious, exalted awakening that he once experienced in his youth, in the days after listening to Gotama's teachings and in the days after parting from Govinda, traveled back to the past. The alert expectation through which he once lived while talking to the Buddha faded into obscurity. The pride of standing alone without teachers and without doctrines that he once realized after leaving the Jetavana Grove sank into oblivion. The eager readiness to listen only to the divine voice within his own heart that he once determined to obey became a memory.

The only sacred fountainhead that had once been near and that had once sung loudly within him now murmured softly in the distance. However, many things that he had learned from the Samanas, that he had heard from Gotama, that he had absorbed from his father, and that he had soaked up from the Brahmins were still retained in his mind. The moderate life, the pleasure in thinking, the hours of meditation, the secret knowledge of the *Self*, and the mystery of the eternal *Self* that was neither the physical body nor the consciousness remained lingering in his psyche for a long time.

Although Siddhartha was still able to retain many things, many others were submerged and covered with dust. Just like the wheel of the potter after being set in motion, it kept on spinning for some time, but it then lost the speed, turned slower in due course, and eventually came to a full stop. This movement pattern of the wheel of the potter was also similar to that of the wheel of the ascetic, to that of the wheel of thinking, and to that of the wheel of discrimination in Siddhartha's soul. All these wheels remained spinning even if at a slow pace; however, hesitantly yet unavoidably, they eventually came to a standstill.

Like moisture that slowly found its way into the dying tree trunk, gradually spread all over the trunk, and eventually rotted the trunk, the material world with inertia and with apathy, little by little, crept into the Siddhartha's soul. At a snail's pace, but surely, it filled his soul; it made his soul feel heavy; it made his soul grow weary; and it sent his soul to sleep. However, at the same time, his six roots of sensations became more awakened. Hence, they learned a great deal and experienced a great deal.

Siddhartha had learned how to transact business affairs, how to exercise power over people, and how to amuse himself with women. He had learned how to wear fine clothes, how to command servants, and how to bathe in the sweet-smelling waters. He had learned how to eat delicacies and how to enjoy carefully prepared food. Fish, meat, and fowl cooked in special spices and baked in delicate dainties became his favorite foods. Drinking wine became one of his routines even though wine made him lazy and forgetful. He had learned how to play dice and chess, how to watch revealing dancers, how to enjoy being carried in sedan chairs, and how to take pleasure in sleeping on a soft bed.

He, however, had always felt that he was different from and was superior to all other people. He had always looked at them through the lens of ridicule, of contempt, and of scorn. The Samanas had always felt this mocking disdain towards the people of the world. When Kamaswami was distraught, was insulted, or was tortured by the business affairs, Siddhartha had often cast a scornful glance at him. However, slowly and imperceptibly, with the passing of the seasons, his mockery towards people and his feeling of superiority over the others diminished.

Gradually, along with the growing riches, Siddhartha, himself, acquired some of the characteristics of the ordinary people, some of their childishness, and some of their anxiety. Yet, he coveted their feelings, coveted their life, and coveted their fate. The more he became like them; the more he envied them. He envied them the one thing that he lacked and that they had.

What was that one thing he lacked?

It was the sense of importance through which they lived their lives. How did they live their lives? They were capable of plunging themselves into both the depth of their pleasures and the depth of their sorrows. They were also capable of binding themselves to the anxious but sweet happiness of their continual power to love. These people were always in love with themselves, with their children, with their honors, with their money, with their plans, and with their hopes. Siddhartha, however, could not learn from them the sense of importance. He could learn neither their childlike pleasures nor their follies. All he could learn from them were the unpleasant things that he, himself, despised.

It happened more frequently that after a merry evening during which Siddhartha engaged in pleasures, he lay late in bed the following morning and felt dull as well as tired.

It also happened more frequently that Siddhartha became annoyed and impatient when Kamaswami bored him with his worries. Now, it became more and more often that Siddhartha laughed too loudly when he lost at dice. His face was still cleverer and more intellectual than those of others were, but he rarely laughed as he often did before. Gradually, his face assumed expressions that had been seen so often on those of the rich. He began to fill his face with expressions of discontent, of weariness, of displeasure, of idleness, and of lovelessness. Slowly but unavoidably, the soul sickness of the rich crept over him.

Like a veil and like a thin mist, a weariness settled on Siddhartha, bit by bit, every day a little thicker, every month a little darker, and every year a little heavier. As a new dress grew old with time, it lost its bright color, and it became stained. Its creases appeared more visible; its hems frayed; its stitches came unraveled; and its threadbare spots started to expose here and there. So did Siddhartha's new life—the life that he had begun after parting from Govinda became old. In the same way, his life lost its color and lost its sheen with the passing of the years. Creases and stains that had been accumulated and had been hidden in the depths of fleeting pleasures now began to reveal themselves here and there. Disillusionment, weariness, and nausea had been waiting to burst open, but Siddhartha was aware of none of them. The only thing, the only one thing that he paid attention to was the bright and clear inward voice. This voice was once awakened in him and was always guided him in the finest hours, but it now became silent. It now uttered nothing.

Life in the material world, indeed, grabbed a hold of Siddhartha. Pleasure, covetousness, idleness, and even acquisitiveness—the vices which he had always despised, scorned, and considered as the most foolish ones—finally backed him into a corner. Property, possessions, and riches, at last, trapped him completely. Every single one of them was no longer a game and no longer a toy to him. They had actually become his chains and his burdens. Through betting and gambling, he had been wandering along a strange path which was full of twists and turns, and unavoidably, he plunged himself down a steep cliff-face at last. The game of dice was the last and the steepest declivity of his path.

Since the time Siddhartha had stopped being a Samana in his heart, he began to play dice for money and for jewels with increasing fervor. Like all ordinary people, the more he played, the more he became passionate about it. At first, as a custom of the ordinary people, he entered the game with an indulgent smile and an easy-going attitude. Not too long thereafter, he became a formidable player. Very, very few people dared to play with him because his stakes were so high and so reckless. He played the game as a result of a heartfelt need. He derived passionate pleasures through gambling away and through squandering of wretched money. In no other way could he show more clearly and mockingly his contempt for the riches and for the false deity of businessmen. For these reasons, he staked high and unsparingly. He tried to avoid being parsimonious, but at the same time, he tried to detest himself and mock himself.

Siddhartha won thousands and threw thousands away. He lost money, lost jewels, and lost his country house. He then won again and lost again. He loved when his chest was throbbing with anxiety. He loved the intense anxiety—the kind of terrible anxiety that he experienced during the game of dice and the kind of oppressive anxiety that he experienced during the suspense of high stakes. He loved these kinds of anxious feelings. He continually sought them, renewed them, increased them, and stimulated them for only in these feelings could he experience some kind of happiness, some kind of excitement, and some kind of heightened living in the midst of his satiated, tepid, and insipid existence.

And after every great loss, he devoted himself to the procurement of new riches, went after the business with more fervor, and pressed his debtors for payment—just because he wanted to play dice again, just because he wanted to squander of wretched money again, and just because he wanted to show his contempt for riches again.

Siddhartha became impatient at losses. He lost his patience with slow-paying debtors. He was no longer kindhearted to beggars. He no longer had the desire to offer loans and to give gifts to the poor. He, who staked ten thousand on the throw of a dice and laughed, became much harder, meaner, and more penny-pinching in business. Worse, he sometimes even dreamt of money at night. And every time whenever he awakened from this hateful spell or whenever he saw his face growing older and uglier in the mirror on the wall of his bedroom or whenever he felt overwhelmed by shame and nausea, he fled. Over and over again, he fled to a new game of chance, fled to passion in confusion, and fled to wine in bewilderment. Then from there, he again threw himself back into the urge of acquiring and hoarding wealth. In this senseless cycle, he let himself being worn out, grew old, and became sick.

Then one day, a dream reminded Siddhartha of something that happened in the past. On one occasion, he was with Kamala in the evening, in her lovely pleasure garden. They sat under a tree talking. Kamala was seriously speaking earnest words behind which grief and weariness were concealed. She asked him to tell her about Gotama, but she could not hear enough about the Illustrious One. Through Siddhartha's words, she imagined how clear and how bright Gotama's eyes were; how peaceful and how beautiful Gotama's mouth was; how gracious and how mysterious Gotama's smile was; and how peaceful and how tranquil Gotama's entire manner was. For a long time, Siddhartha had to tell her about the Illustrious Buddha.

Kamala released a long sigh and said, "One day, perhaps soon, I will also become a follower of this Buddha. I will bestow upon him my pleasure garden and take refuge in his teachings." However, she then enticed Siddhartha, and in a passionate love-play, she clasped him to her with an extreme fervor fiercely and tearfully. It was as if she wanted to extract the last sweet drop from this fleeting pleasure one more time. Never had it been so strangely clear to Siddhartha that how closely related passion was to death.

Siddhartha then lay beside her, and Kamala's face was near to his. Under her eyes and near the corners of her mouth, he clearly read a sad sign for the first time. Fine lines and wrinkles indicated the signs that gave a reminder of autumn and old age. Siddhartha, himself, who was only in his forties, had noticed gray hairs here and there in his black hair. Weariness was written on Kamala's beautiful face. Her weariness was perhaps from walking along a lengthy path that had no joyous goal.

Their weariness, their incipient old age, and their fear had long been concealed in each of them, but neither of them had mentioned any of theirs. Perhaps, they both had not quite yet become conscious of fears—fear of the autumn of life, fear of old age, and fear of death.

While sighing, Siddhartha took leave of Kamala, but his heart was full of misery and secret fears.

On that same night, Siddhartha spent the rest of the time in his own house with dancers and wine. He still presumed that he was superior to his companions even though, in reality, he no longer was. He drank much wine and did not go to bed until much later after midnight. Although he was tired, he kept tossing and turning. He was nearly in tears and was on the brink of total despair. In vain, he tried to fall asleep. His heart was so full of misery that he felt he could no longer endure anything anymore.

Siddhartha felt as if the nausea overpowered him. This nauseated feeling was like the distasteful wine, was like the superficial music, was like the too sweet smile of the dancers, and was like the overwhelming smell of the perfume from their hair and their breasts. However, above all, he was nauseated with himself, with the perfume from his own hair, with the smell of wine from his own mouth, and with the flabby appearance of his own skin. Like someone who ate so much and drank so much that he had to end up vomiting everything painfully in order to feel better afterward, the restless spirit in Siddhartha wished that he could rid himself with one terrific heave of these pleasures, of these habits, and of this entirely senseless life.

Until the daybreak, when the first signs of activities outside Siddhartha's town house began, he started dozing off, passed gracefully into a few moments of semi-oblivion, and finally fell asleep. During this time, he had a dream.

Kamala kept a little rare songbird in a small golden cage. It was about this little bird that he dreamt. This bird, which usually sang in the morning, unexpectedly became mute. As this silence surprised him, he went up to the cage and looked inside. The little bird was dead and lay stiff on the floor. He took it out, held it for a moment in his hand, and then threw it away on the road. At that same moment, he was suddenly horrified, and his heart ached. He felt as if everything that was good and was of value in him was thrown away together with the dead bird.

After waking up from this dream, Siddhartha was overwhelmed by a feeling of great sadness. It seemed to him that he had spent his life in a worthless and senseless manner. He retained nothing vital, nothing precious, and nothing worthwhile. He stood alone, like a shipwrecked man on the shore.

Sadly, Siddhartha went to the pleasure garden that belonged to him. He closed the gates and sat under a mango tree. He felt as if his heart was filled with horror and death. While sitting underneath this mango tree, he felt himself dying, withering, and finishing. Gradually, he emotionally collected his thoughts and mentally went through the whole of his life, starting from the earliest days that he could remember.

When had Siddhartha really been happy? When had Siddhartha really experienced joy? Well, Siddhartha had been happy and had experienced joy many times. He had tasted happiness's in the days of his boyhood when he won praise from the Brahmins and when he far out-stripped his contemporaries. He had felt a great joy in his heart when he excelled himself at the recitation of the holy verses, when he took part in the learned men's conversations, and when he assisted to offer sacrifices to the gods. At those moments, he heard the voice of his heart, "A path lies before you. You are called to follow it, and the gods await you."

Again, as a youth, he had felt happy when his soaring goal continually propelled him in and out of the crowd of similar seekers and when he strove hard to understand the Brahmins' teachings. He had felt a great joy in his heart whenever e fresh acquired knowledge engendered a new thirst. Then in the midst of his thirst and in the midst of his effort, he had again heard the same voice of his heart, "Move onwards. Move onwards. Move onwards. This is your path." Yet again, he had heard this same voice after he left his father's home to live the life of the Samana. Once more, he had heard this same voice after he left the Samana to go to the Perfect One. Yet another time, he had heard this same voice when he left the Illustrious One to follow the unknown.

How long was it since Siddhartha had last heard this voice? How long was it now since he had last soared to any height? How flat, how desolate, and how gloomy his path had been! How many long years he had spent his life with no lofty goal, with no new thirst, and with no exaltation! How many long years he had spent his life while feeling content with small pleasures! How many long years he had spent his life while never once actually feeling satisfied!

Although Siddhartha did not know exactly what could bring him satisfaction, he had craved for being satisfied and had made a tremendous effort all these years. He had longed for being like all others and had longed for being like the childlike people. Yet, his life was still much more wretched and was still much poorer than theirs were.

What he did not realize was that their aims were not like his, and their sorrows were not like his. The whole world of the Kamaswami people had only been a game for him to play, and the whole world of the dancers and other passing pleasures had only been a comedy for him to watch. To him, they all were nothing more than just fleeting shows.

Only was Kamala dear to Siddhartha—had been of value to him—but was she still? Did he still need her, and did she still need him? Were they not playing a game without an end? Was it necessary for both of them to keep going for a game like such? No, it was not necessary for both of them to live for such a game. This game was called Samsara—a game for children. It was a game that was perhaps enjoyable to play once, twice, or ten times, but was it worth playing continually?

Siddhartha then realized that the game was finished and that he could play it no longer. A shudder passed through his body, and he felt as if something just died.

For the rest of that day, Siddhartha remained sitting under the mango tree, thinking of his father, thinking of Govinda, and thinking of Gotama. Had he left all of them in order to become a Kamaswami?

He sat there until the night fell. When he looked up and saw the stars, he mumbled, "I am sitting here under my mango tree, in my pleasure garden." He smiled a little and talked to himself, "Is it necessary, Siddhartha? Is it right, Siddhartha? Is it not a foolish thing that Siddhartha should possess a mango tree and a pleasure garden?"

Siddhartha was so tired of everything in this world. He had finished with everything, and everything had died in his heart. He rose and said farewell to both, to the mango tree and to the pleasure garden. As he had not had any food that day, he felt extremely hungry. He immediately thought of his house in the town, thought of his room, thought of his bed, and thought of the table with food. He smiled wearily, shook his head, and said good-bye to all these things as well.

On that same night, Siddhartha left his garden, left the town, and never returned. For a long time, Kamaswami tried to find Siddhartha and eventually believed that he had already fallen into the hands of bandits.

Kamala, in contrast, did not even try to find Siddhartha. She was not at all surprised when she learned that he had disappeared. Had she not always expected it? Was he not a Samana without a home? Was he not a pilgrim without a destination? She had fully realized and had clearly felt who he actually was more than ever at their last meeting. However, in the midst of her pain brought about by her loss, she rejoiced that she had pressed him so close to her heart on that last occasion. She also rejoiced that he was completely possessed by her, and she was completely mastered by him.

When Kamala heard the first news of Siddhartha's disappearance, she went to the window where she kept the rare songbird in the golden cage. She opened the door of the cage, took the bird out, and let it fly away. For a long time, she stood still and looked at the bird disappearing in plain sight. From that day, she received no more visitors and kept her house closed. A little while later, she found that she was with a child as a result of her last meeting with Siddhartha.

Remark: Siddhartha's third awakening—Leaving the material life altogether was Siddhartha's third awakening. After indulging himself in a luxurious living and entertaining himself with sensual passions, he became awakened that he gained nothing other than weariness, nausea, and disillusionment but lost so much.

CHAPTER 8

BY THE RIVER

Siddhartha wandered into the forest that was already far from the town. He now only knew one thing, and that was he could not go back. The life he had been living for many years was past. He had tasted everything and had drained everything to a degree of nausea. The songbird was dead, and its death about which he dreamt was the bird in his own heart. He was deeply entangled in Samsara. He had drawn nausea and death from all sides to himself. It was like a sponge that absorbed much water until it was completely full. He was full of ennui, full of misery, and full of death. There was nothing in the world that could attract him, could bring him pleasure, and could give him solace.

Siddhartha wished passionately that he could be oblivious, be at rest, and be dead! He wishes that a flash of lightning would strike him! He wished that a tiger would come and eat him! He wished that there were some kind of wine or some kind of poison that would make him become oblivious, would make him forget, and would make him fall asleep without waking up ever again!

Was there any kind of filth that Siddhartha had not besmirched himself? Were there any sin and any folly in his soul that he had not committed? Was there any stain in his soul for which he himself was not responsible? Was it then still possible to live? Was it still possible to breathe in, to breathe out, to feel hungry, to eat, to sleep, and to lie with women again and again? Was this cycle not exhausted and finished for him?

Siddhartha reached the longest river in the wood. It was the same river that the ferryman once took him across when he was still a young man who just left the Jetavana garden of Gotama. He stopped at this river and stood hesitatingly on the bank. Fatigue and hunger made him feel weak and tired. Why was he supposed to keep on going? Where was he supposed to go and for what purpose? There was no more purpose. There was nothing more than just a deep, painful longing to shake off this completely confused dream, to spit out this stale wine, and to end this bitter, painful life.

There was a tree on the river bank, a coconut tree. Siddhartha leaned against the trunk, wrapped his arms around it, and looked down into the green water that flowed beneath him. While looking down into the water, he was completely filled with a desire to let himself go and to let himself be submerged in the water. A chilly emptiness in the water reflected the terrible emptiness in his soul. Yes, he was at the end. There was nothing more for him to do but to efface himself, to destroy the unsuccessful structure of his life, to throw it away, and to be mocked at by the gods. Those were the deeds, which he longed to commit. He longed to destroy the form that he hated! Might the fish devour him—this ugly dog Siddhartha; this madman; this corrupted, rotting body; and this sluggish, misused soul! Might the fish consume him. Might the crocodiles grind him. Might the demons tear him to little pieces.

With a strangely distorted countenance, he stared into the water. He saw his face reflected and spat at it. He took one of his arms away from the tree trunk and turned his body a little so that he could fall headlong and finally go under. With closed eyes, he bent down low as if he looked towards death.

Then from a remote part of his soul and from the past of his tired life, he suddenly heard a sound reverberated. It was one word, a syllable, that, without thinking, he spoke indistinctly. It was the ancient beginning and ending of all Brahmin prayers, the "Om", which had the meaning of "the Awakened One" or "the Perfect One". At that very moment, when the sound of the "Om" reached his ears, his slumbering soul suddenly awakened, and he recognized the folly of his action.

Siddhartha was deeply horrified; therefore, that was how he turned out in the end. He was so lost, so confused, and so devoid of all reasons that he had to seek death. This wish, this childish wish had grown so strong in him that he wanted to find peace by destroying his own body. It was apparent that not all the torments of these recent times, all the disillusionment, and all the despair had affected him as much as the moment when the "Om" reached his consciousness. At that moment, he recognized his wretchedness and his crime.

"Om," he pronounced inwardly. He was then conscious of Brahmin and of the indestructibleness of life. He recalled all that he had forgotten and all things that were divine.

However, it was only for a moment, a flash. Siddhartha sank down at the foot of the coconut tree because the fatigue completely defeated him. Whilst murmuring Om, he laid his head on the tree roots and sank into a deep sleep.

His sleep was deep and dreamless. He had not slept like that for a long time. When he woke up after many hours of sleep, it seemed to him that ten years had passed. He heard the soft ripples of the water, but he knew neither where he was nor what brought him here. He looked up and was surprised to see the trees and the sky above him. He then remembered where he was and how he came here. He felt a desire to remain here for a long time. At this point in time, to him, the past seemed to be covered by a veil, seemed to be extremely remote, and seemed to be very unimportant. He only knew that his previous life (at the very first moment of his return to consciousness, his previous life, to him, seemed like a remote incarnation or seemed like an earlier birth of his present *Self*) was finished. It was so full of nausea and wretchedness that he wanted to destroy it. However, he came to himself by a river, under a coconut tree, and with the holy word Om on his lips. He then fell asleep, and on awakening, he looked at the world as if he was a new man. Softly, he said the word Om to himself. It seemed as if he fell asleep with the word Om and seemed as if throughout his entire long, deep sleep, he was reciting Om, was thinking of Om, and was emerging into Om. All together, he was penetrating into Om, into the nameless, and into the Divine.

What a wonderful sleep it was! Never did a sleep make him feel so refreshed, so renewed, and so rejuvenated! Perhaps, he actually died. Perhaps, he was drowned and was reborn in another form. But no, he recognized himself. He recognized his own hands and his own feet. He recognized the place where he lay and recognized the breast where his own *Self* dwelt. He, Siddhartha, was a self-willed individualist. However, this Siddhartha was somewhat changed and somewhat renewed. He had a wonderful sleep. He was now remarkably awake, happy, and curious before everything.

Siddhartha raised himself and saw a monk in a yellow gown with a shaved head sitting opposite him in the attitude of a thinker. He looked at the monk who had neither hair on his head nor a beard on his chin, and not before long, he recognized that this monk was Govinda, the friend of his youth, who had taken refuge in the Illustrious Buddha. Govinda had also aged, but his face still carried the old characteristics—eagerness, loyalty, curiosity, and anxiety. However, when Govinda expressed his feeling through his gaze toward the man who raised his eyes and looked at him, Siddhartha realized that Govinda did not recognize him. Govinda was pleased to find the man awake. Apparently, Govinda had been sitting beside the man for a long time and had been waiting for the man to awaken even though he did not know whom the man was.

"I was sleeping," said Siddhartha. "How did you come here?"

"You were sleeping," answered Govinda. "Seriously, it is not good to sleep in such places where snakes and animals from the forest often prowl around in search of food. I am one of the followers of the Illustrious Gotama, the Buddha of Sakyamuni, and I am on a pilgrimage with a number of brothers of our order. I saw you lying asleep in a dangerous place, so I tried to awaken you. Then when I saw you were sleeping very deeply, I decided to remain behind my brothers and sat by you. Then it seems that I who want to watch over you fell asleep myself. Weariness overcame me, and I kept my watch badly. Now that you are awake, so I must go and try to catch up with my brothers."

"I thank you, the Samana, for guarding my sleep," said Siddhartha, "The followers of the Illustrious One are very kind, but now you may go on your way."

"I am going," smiled Govinda, "May you keep well."

"I thank you, the Samana," Siddhartha waved his hand.

Govinda bowed and said, "Good-bye."

"Good-bye, Govinda," said Siddhartha.

The monk stood still.

"Excuse me, Sir, how do you know my name?" startled Govinda.

Thereupon, Siddhartha laughed.

"I know you, Govinda, from your father's house, from the Brahmins' school, from the sacrifices, from our sojourn with the Samanas, and at the hours in the Jetavana Grove where you swore your allegiance to the Illustrious One."

"You are Siddhartha," cried Govinda aloud. "Now, I recognize you, and I do not understand why I did not recognize you immediately. Greetings, Siddhartha! It gives me great pleasure to see you again."

"I am also pleased to see you again," said Siddhartha. "You have watched over me during my sleep. I thank you, once again, although I needed no guard. Where are you going, my friend?"

"I am not going anywhere," said Govinda, "We, the monks, are always on the way except during the rainy season. We always move from place to place, live according to the rules, preach the gospel, collect alms, and then move on. It is always the same. But where are you going, Siddhartha?"

Siddhartha said, "It is the same with me as it is with you, my friend. I am not going anywhere. I am only on the way. I am making a pilgrimage."

Govinda said, "You say that you are making a pilgrimage, and I believe you. However, forgive me, Siddhartha, you do not look like a pilgrim. You are wearing the clothes of a rich man. You are wearing the shoes of a fashionable man. And your perfumed hair is neither the hair of a pilgrim nor the hair of a Samana."

"You observe very well, my friend," smiled Siddhartha. "You see everything with your sharp eyes, but I did not tell you that I am a Samana, did I? I said that I am making a pilgrimage, and that is true."

"You are making a pilgrimage," said Govinda, "but very few people make a pilgrimage in such clothes, in such shoes, and with such hair. I have wandered around for many years, but I have never once seen such a pilgrim."

"I believe you, Govinda," said Siddhartha with a gentle smile, "but today, you have met such a pilgrim who is in such clothes, in such shoes, and with such hair. Remember, my dear Govinda, the world of appearances is transitory. The style of our clothes and the style of our hair are extremely transitory. Our hair and our body are themselves transitory. You have observed correctly. I am wearing the clothes of a rich man and wearing the shoes of a fashionable man. I am wearing them because I have been a rich man. I am wearing my hair like men of the temporal world and like men of the fashion trends because I have been one of them."

"And what are you now, Siddhartha?" surprisingly asked Govinda.

"I do not know. I know as little as you do," said Siddhartha. "I am only on the way. I was a rich man, but I am now no longer a rich man. And what will I be tomorrow? I do not know."

"Have you lost your riches?" asked Govinda with concern.

"I lost them, or they lost me—I am not sure," replied Siddhartha with a shrug. "The wheel of appearances revolves very quickly, Govinda. Where is Siddhartha, the Brahmin? Where is Siddhartha, the Samana? Where is Siddhartha, the rich man? The transitory soon changes, Govinda. You know that."

For a long time, Govinda looked doubtfully at the friend of his youth. He then bowed to Siddhartha as if he did to a man of rank and went on his way.

While smiling, Siddhartha watched his friend go. He still loved Govinda, his faithful yet anxious friend. And at that moment, in that splendid hour, after his wonderful sleep, permeated with Om, how could he help but love everybody and everything. That was just the magic that had happened to him while he was sleeping with the holy Om in him. He loved everything. He was full of joyous love towards everything that he saw. And he now seemed to perceive the reason that made him feel miserable in the past. He felt so ill because he could love no one and could love nothing.

With a smile, Siddhartha watched the departing monk, the friend of his youth. The deep sleep had strengthened him, but he suffered great hunger because he had not eaten anything for two days. The time that he could ward off hunger was long past. Troubled and yet with laughter, he recalled that time. He remembered back at that time, he boasted of three things to Kamala. He was so proud of his three noble and invincible arts, "Thinking, waiting, and fasting."

He considered these arts as his possessions, his power, and his strength. He learned these three arts and nothing else during the diligent, assiduous years of his youth. Now, he lost them all. He possessed none of them. Thinking, waiting, and fasting were no longer his possessions, his power, and his strength. He had exchanged them for the most wretched things, for the transitory possessions, for the pleasures of the senses, for the high living, and for the riches. He had gone along a strange path, and now, it seemed that he had indeed become an ordinary person.

Siddhartha reflected on his state. He found that it was so difficult for him to think. In fact, he really had no desire to, but he forced himself.

He mumbled to himself, "Now that all these transitory things have slipped away from me. Again, I stand beneath the sun as I once did when I was a young child. Nothing is mine; I know nothing; I learn nothing; and I possess nothing. How strange it is! Now, when I am no longer young, when my hair is fast growing gray, and when my strength begins to diminish, I am beginning again to live as if I was a child."

He then smiled again. Yes, his destiny was strange, indeed! He was going backwards. Now, he again stood empty, was again naked, and was again ignorant in the world. He, however, did not grieve because of all that. On the contrary, he even felt a great desire to laugh, to laugh with him, and to laugh with this strange foolish world!

"Things are going backwards with you," he said to himself and laughed aloud. And when he said it, his gaze lighted on the river. He then saw the river also flowing continually backwards and singing merrily. What he saw pleased him immensely, and he smiled cheerfully with the river. Was this not the river in which he once wished to drown himself? How long ago was it? Was it hundreds of years ago, or was it just his dream?

"How strange my life has been?" whispered Siddhartha, "I have wandered along many strange paths. When I was a boy, the gods and sacrifices always occupied my mind. When I became a youth, I was passionately fond of meditation and asceticism. I was in search of Brahmin and revered the eternal in the Atman. When I turned into a young man, I was attracted to expiation. I lived in the woods, suffered the heat, and endured the cold. I learned to fast, and I learned to conquer my body. I then discovered wonderful teachings of the great Buddha. I felt that knowledge and the unity of the universe circulated inside of me like my own blood, but by the same token, I also felt compelled that I needed to leave the Buddha and the great knowledge. I went and learned the pleasures of love from Kamala and transactions of business from Kamaswami. I hoarded money, and I then squandered money. I acquired a taste of rich food, and I learned to simulate my six roots of sensations. I had to spend many years of my life like that in order to lose my intelligence, to lose my power of thinking, and to forget about the unity of things. Is it not true that slowly and through many deviations, I have changed from a man into a child and from a thinker into an ordinary person? Yet, this path has been useful, and the bird in my breast has not died. However, what a path it has been! I have had to experience so much stupidity, so many vices, so many errors, so much nausea, so many disillusionments, and so many sorrows just in order to become a child again. However, it is right that it should be so. My eyes and my heart have acclaimed them all. I have to experience despair; I have to sink into the greatest mental depths; and I have to survive my suicidal thought in order to experience grace again, to hear Om again, to sleep deeply again, and to awaken refreshed again. I have to become a fool again in order to find Atman in myself. I have to sin in order to live again. Whither will my path yet lead me? This path is stupid for it goes in spirals. Perhaps, it goes in circles, but regardless of whichever way it goes, I will follow it."

He felt a great happiness mounting within him.

"From where does this great happiness come?" Siddhartha asked himself. "What is the reason for this feeling of great happiness? Does it arise from my good long sleep that has made me feel so much better? Does it come from the world Om that I pronounced? Does it come because I have run away and because my flight has been accomplished? Does it come because I am, at last, free again and because I, once again, stand like a child beneath the sky? Oh, how good it is to experience this accomplished flight and how good it is to feel liberated! In the place from which I have escaped, there is always an atmosphere of pomade, of spice, of excess, and of inertia. Oh, how I hate that world of riches, of the revels, and of compulsive gamblers! Oh, how I hate myself for remaining so long in that horrible world! Oh, how I hate myself for distorting the facts, for poisoning myself, for torturing myself, for making myself get old, and making myself become ugly. Never again will I consider that Siddhartha is intelligent as I once proudly imagined. But one thing, I have done well, which pleases me and makes me praise myself is that I have now put an end to the self-detestation and to the foolish empty life. I commend you, Siddhartha, that after so many years of folly, you have had a beautiful thought; you have accomplished something; and you have again heard the bird in your breast sing and decide to follow it.

Hence, he praised himself and was pleased with himself, but at the same time, he listened curiously to his stomach that rumbled from hunger. He felt that he thoroughly tasted, digested, and finally ejected a portion of sorrow and a portion of misery during those past times and that he consumed them to the point of despair and of death. But all was well.

He could have remained much longer with Kamaswami to make money and squander it and to feed his body and neglect his soul. He could have dwelt in that soft, well-upholstered hell for even a longer time if he had not experienced moments of complete hopelessness and the tense moment when he bent over the flowing waters and was ready to commit suicide.

In spite of everything, the despair, the complete hopelessness, the tense moment, and the extreme nausea that he experienced did not overpower him. The bird, the clear spring, and the voice within him were still alive. The fact that they were all still alive explained why he rejoiced, why he laughed, and why his face was radiant under his gray hair.

"It is a good thing to experience everything oneself," he talked to himself. "As a child, I learned that the pleasures of the world and riches were not good. I have known them for a long time, but I have only just experienced them. Now, I know them not only with my intellect but also with my eyes, with my heart, and with my stomach. It is a good thing that I know them from real life experiences."

He thought long about the change in him and listened to the bird within him singing happily at the same time. If the bird within him had died, would he have perished? No, the bird within him had not died. Something else in him had died. Something that he had long desired had finally perished. What was that something? Was it not what he had once wished to destroy during his ardent years of asceticism? Was it not his *Self*—his small, fearful, and proud *Self*—against which he had wrestled for so many years? Was it not the *Self* that always conquered him, that always appeared each time again and again, that always robbed him of his happiness, and that always filled him with fear? Was it not the *Self* that finally died today in the wood by this delightful river? Was it not because of its death that he was now like a child who was so full of trust and was so full happiness without fear?

Siddhartha now also realized why he struggled in vain with his *Self* when he was a Brahmin and an ascetic. Too much knowledge hindered him. Too many holy verses, too many sacrificial rites, too much mortification of the flesh, too much doing, and too much striving held him back. He was always full of arrogance. He was always the cleverest and the most eager Brahmin. He was always a step ahead of all others. He was always the learned, intellectual one. He was always the priest or the sage. His *Self* crawled into his priesthood, crawled into his arrogance, and crawled into his intellectuality.

Wherever it crawled into, it sat there firmly and grew wildly while he thought he was in the process of destroying it by fasting and penitence. He now understood his *Self* and realized that his inward voice had always been right. The voice had always asserted him that no teacher could have brought him salvation. That was why he had to go into the world and had to lose himself not only in power and in woman but also in money and in riches. That was also why he had to be a merchant, why he had to be a dice player, why he had to be a drinker, and why he had to be a man of property. He had to be all these people so that the priest and the Samana in him were dead. That was why he had to undergo those horrible years, had to suffer nausea, and had to learn lessons about the madness of an empty yet futile life not only until the end but also until he reached bitter despair so that Siddhartha, the pleasure-monger, and Siddhartha, the man of property, could die. He died, but a new Siddhartha had awakened from his long, deep sleep.

Like everybody else, the new Siddhartha would grow old and would die as well. Siddhartha was transitory. All forms of Siddhartha were transitory, but today, the new Siddhartha was young. He was a child and was very happy.

These thoughts passed through his mind. While smiling, he listened to his stomach and listened thankfully to a humming bee. Happily, he looked into the flowing river. Never had a river attracted his attention as much as this one! Never had he found the voice of the water and the appearance of the flowing water so beautiful! It seemed as if the river had something special to tell him, had something unknown to him, and had something waiting for him.

The old Siddhartha once wanted to drown himself in this river, so the aged, tired, despairing Siddhartha was today drowned in it.

The new Siddhartha felt a deep love for this flowing water and decided that he would not leave it again so quickly.

Remark: Siddhartha's fourth awakening—Abandoning the suicidal thought was Siddhartha's fourth awakening. After surviving the commit suicide, he became awakened that nothing in the material world could affect him more than the sacred sound "Om" reverberated from the most isolated part of his soul.

CHAPTER 9

THE FERRYMAN

"I will remain by this river," mumbled Siddhartha. "It is the same river which I crossed on my way to the town. A friendly ferryman took me across. I will go to him. The path, which I was on in the past, once led me from his hut to a new life, but now, that path is old and dead. May the present path, my new life, start from here!"

Lovingly, he looked into the flowing river, looked into the transparent green, and looked into the crystal lines of the wonderful design. He saw bright pearls rise from the depths, saw bubbles swim on the mirror, and saw the blue sky reflect on the bubbles. The river looked at him with hundreds of thousands of eyes—green, white, crystal, and sky blue. How he loved this river! How it enchanted him! How grateful he was to it!

In his heart, he heard the newly awakened voice speak, and it said to him, "Love this river, stay by it, and learn from it." Yes, he wanted to learn from it. He wanted to listen to it. It seemed to him that if whoever understood this river and its secrets, that person would understand much more, many secrets, and all secrets.

But today, he only saw one of the river's secrets, and this one had gripped his soul. He saw that the water continually flowed and flowed, and yet, it was always there. It was always the same before his eyes, and yet, it was new at every moment.

Who could understand and perceive this notion? Siddhartha could not. He could only sense a dim suspicion, a faint memory, and divine voices.

Siddhartha rose. The pangs of hunger were becoming unbearable. He painfully wandered along the river bank, listened to the rippling of the water, and listened to the gnawing hunger in his body.

When he reached the ferry, the boat was already there, and the ferryman who once took the young Samana across the river stood in the boat. Siddhartha immediately recognized him who was also aged very much.

"Will you take me across the river?" asked Siddhartha.

The ferryman, who was astonished to see such a distinguished-looking man alone and on foot, invited the man into the boat and set off.

"You have chosen a splendid life," said Siddhartha. "It must be very gratifying to live near this river and sail on it every day."

The rower swayed the boat gently and smiled, "Indeed, it is very rewarding, Sir, as you said, but is not every life or every work enjoyable?"

"Maybe, but I envy you yours," replied Siddhartha.

"Oh, you may soon lose your taste for it. It is not for the people who are in fine clothes," smiled the ferryman.

Siddhartha laughed, "I have already been judged by my clothes today and have been regarded with suspicion. Will you accept these clothes, which I find them nothing but a nuisance, from me? I must tell you that I have no money to pay you for taking me across the river."

"The gentleman is joking," laughed the ferryman aloud.

"I am not joking, my friend," said Siddhartha seriously. "In the past, you once took me across this river without payment, so would you please do it today also and take my clothes instead?"

"And will the gentleman continue without clothes?" asked the ferryman smiled.

"I would prefer not to go any further," said Siddhartha. "I would prefer it if you could give me some old clothes and keep me here as your assistant. It would be even better if you could keep me here as your apprentice for I must learn from you how to handle the boat."

The ferryman looked keenly at the stranger for a long time. "I recognize you," he said finally. "You once slept in my hut. It was a long time ago. Maybe it was more than twenty years ago. I took you across the river, and we parted from each other like good friends. Were you not a Samana back then? I am sorry that I cannot remember your name."

"My name is Siddhartha," replied Siddhartha with a smile, "and yes, I was a Samana when you last saw me."

"It is my great pleasure to greet you again, Siddhartha," said the ferryman merrily, "My name is Vasudeva. I hope that you will be my guest today and will sleep in my hut. I also hope that this time, you will tell me where you have come from and why you are so tired of your fine clothes."

When they had reached the middle of the river, Vasudeva had to work much harder because he rowed against the current. He, however, rowed calmly. With strong arms, he kept the boat moving forward steadily while his eyes fixed in on the front of the boat.

Siddhartha sat quietly and watched Vasudeva. He remembered how once, in those last Samana days, he had a very fond affection for this ferryman.

When they reached the river bank, Siddhartha helped Vasudeva to secure the boat and gratefully accepted his invitation.

Vasudeva then led Siddhartha into his hut where he offered Siddhartha bread, water, and the mango fruit that Siddhartha ate with enjoyment.

A little while later, when the sun was beginning to set, they sat on a tree trunk by the river. Siddhartha started telling Vasudeva about his origin and about his life, which were from a boy to the hour of despair and to the moment he met the ferryman again today. The story lasted late into the night.

Vasudeva listened with great attention. He heard all about Siddhartha's origin and Siddhartha's childhood. He also heard all about Siddhartha's study, Siddhartha's seek, Siddhartha's pleasures, and Siddhartha's needs. One of the ferryman's greatest virtues that very few people had was the art of listening. He knew how to listen and not utter a word. Siddhartha, the storyteller, felt that Vasudeva carefully took in every word in silence, and with great interest, Vasudeva attentively listened as if he missed nothing. Vasudeva did not await anything with impatience and gave neither praise nor blame—he only listened. Siddhartha felt so wonderful to know such a listener like Vasudeva who could be absorbed into his life, into his strivings, and into his sorrows.

However, toward the end of Siddhartha's story, when he told Vasudeva about the ancient tree by the river, about his deep despair, about the holy Om, and about how he felt such a love for the river after his long, deep sleep,

Vasudeva listened to the story with doubled attention, completely absorbed, his eyes closed.

When Siddhartha finished his story, there was a long pause thereupon.

Vasudeva said, "It is just as I thought. The river spoke to you itself. It is friendly toward you. It speaks to you. That is good, very good! Stay with me, Siddhartha, my friend. I once had a wife. Her bed was by the side of mine, but she died long ago. I have lived alone for a long time. Come and live with me. There are room and food for both of us."

"I thank you," said Siddhartha, "I thank you and gratefully accept your invitation. I also thank you, Vasudeva, for listening to my story so well! There are very few people who know how to listen, and I have never met anybody who can listen as well as you can. I will also learn from you in this respect."

"You will learn how to listen," said Vasudeva, "but not from me. The river has taught me how to listen. It will teach you, too, and you will learn from it. The river knows everything, and everyone can learn everything from it. You have already learned from the river that it is good to strive downwards and to sink deep in order to seek the depths. You also have already learned from the river that the learned Brahmin, the rich man, and the distinguished looking man, Siddhartha, will become a rower and then will become a ferryman. Hitherto, you have already learned a few things from the river. You will learn many other things from the river, too."

After a long pause, Siddhartha asked, "What are other things, Vasudeva?"

Vasudeva rose. "It has grown late," he said, "let us go to bed. I cannot tell you what other things are, my friend. You will soon find out. Perhaps, you already know. I am not a learned man. I do not know how to talk and how to think. I only know how to listen and how to be devout. Besides these two things, I know nothing else. If I could talk and teach, I would perhaps be a teacher. But as it is, I am only a ferryman, and my task is to take people across this river. I have taken thousands of people across, and to almost all of them, my river has been nothing but a hindrance in their journey. Regardless of whether they travelled for money, for business, for a wedding, or for a pilgrimage, the river has always been in their way, and the ferryman is just there to take them quickly across their obstacle. However, amongst the thousands, there have been a few, four or five, to whom the river is not their obstacle. They have heard the voice of the river and have listened to it. Thereafter, the river has become holy to them as it has become to me. Let us now go to bed, Siddhartha."

Siddhartha stayed with the ferryman and learned how to look after the boat. When there was nothing to do at the ferry, he worked in the rice field with Vasudeva. He helped Vasudeva gather wood and pick fruit from the banana trees. He learned from Vasudeva how to make oars, how to improve the boat, and how to make baskets. He was pleased with everything he did and pleased with everything he learned.

As the days and the months passed quickly, he learned more from the river than Vasudeva could ever teach him. He continuously learned from the river every day. Above all, he learned from it how to listen—listen with a still heart, listen with patience, and listen with an opened soul. Most importantly, he learned from it how to listen with no passion, with no desire, with no judgment, and with no opinion.

He lived happily with Vasudeva, and occasionally, they exchanged words. Their exchanges were few and long considered words because Vasudeva was no friend of words. He was rarely successful in moving Vasudeva to speak.

One day, he asked Vasudeva, "Have you also learned from the river that there is no such thing called time?"

A bright smile spread over the Vasudeva's face.

"Yes, Siddhartha," said Vasudeva cheerfully. "Do you mean that the river is everywhere at the same time? Do you mean that the river is at the source, at the mouth, at the waterfall, at the ferry, at the current, in the ocean, and in the mountains? Do you mean that the river is everywhere all at once? Do you mean that the river only exists in the present time? Do you mean that the river is neither the shadow of the past nor the shadow of the future?"

"That is it," said Siddhartha, "After I learned that from the river, I reviewed my life and realized that my life is just like a river. All—Siddhartha the boy, Siddhartha the mature man, and Siddhartha the old man—were only separated from each other by the shadows, not by the reality. Siddhartha's previous lives were not in the past. Siddhartha's future death and Siddhartha's future return to Brahmin are not in the future. Nothing was; everything is; and nothing will be.

Everything has reality and presence."

Siddhartha spoke with delight. The discovery of no such thing called time made him feel very happy. Were then not all sorrows in time? Were then not all self-torments in time? Were then not all fears were in time? Were not all difficulties and all evils in the world conquered as soon as one conquered time or as soon as one dispelled time?

Siddhartha spoke with delight, but Vasudeva just nodded his agreement and smiled radiantly with him. He then stroked the Siddhartha's shoulder and returned to his work.

On a different occasion, when the river swelled and roared loudly during the rainy season, Siddhartha said, "Is it true, my friend, that the river has many voices? Does it have the voice of a king, the voice of a warrior, the voice of a bull, the voice of a night bird, the voice of a pregnant woman, the voice of a sighing man, and a thousand other voices?"

"Yes, it is so," nodded Vasudeva, "the voices of all living creatures are in its voice."

"And do you know," continued Siddhartha, "what word the river pronounces when someone is successful in hearing all of its ten thousand voices at the same time?"

Vasudeva laughed joyously. He stooped towards Siddhartha and whispered the holy Om in Siddhartha's ear. "Om" was just what Siddhartha heard.

As time went on, Siddhartha's smile began to resemble the ferryman's smile. It was almost equally radiant, almost equally full of happiness, almost equally lighting up through a thousand little wrinkles, almost equally childish, and almost equally senile.

Many travelers, when seeing both ferrymen together, took them for brothers.

Very often, the two old friends sat together on the tree trunk by the river in the evening. They both silently listened to the sound of the water that, to them, was not just the sound of the water, but that was rather the voice of life, the voice of being, or the voice of perpetual Becoming.

And it sometimes happened that while listening to the river, they both thought of the same thoughts—either of their conversation from the previous day, of one of the travelers whose fate and circumstances occupied their minds, of death, or of their childhood. When the river told both of them about something good at the same moment, they looked at each other and smiled with each other. They both were thinking of the same thoughts and were happy with the same answer to the same question.

Many travelers felt that something emanated from the ferry and from both ferrymen. It sometimes happened that a traveler, after looking at the face of one of the ferrymen, began to tell the story of his own life, to talk about his troubles, to confess his sins, to seek comfort, and then to ask for advice. It sometimes happened that someone asked the ferrymen for permission to spend an evening with them in order to listen to the river.

It also happened that curious people came along because they heard from rumors that two wise men at the ferry might have been two magicians or two holy men. These curious people asked the ferrymen many questions, but they received no answers. They found neither magicians nor wise men at the ferry. They only found two friendly old men who appeared to be mute. In other words, they only met two strange yet stupid old men. They then laughed aloud and talked with each other about how foolish and how credulous people were for spreading such wild rumors.

The years passed, and nobody regarded the two old friends at the ferry. Then, one day, some monks, the followers of Gotama—the Buddha, came along and asked to be taken across the river. The ferrymen learned from the monks that they were returning to their great teacher as quickly as possible. They were in a great hurry because the news had spread that the Illustrious One was seriously ill. He was about to experience his last mortal death and to attain salvation.

Not long afterwards, another party of monks arrived, and then another appeared at the ferry. All the monks and most of the travelers talked of nothing but Gotama and his approaching mortal death. Like coming to a military expedition or coming to the crowning of a king, people from all sides gathered akin to swarming bees clustered on a tree limb or tiny pieces of metals being drawn by a magnet. They all travelled towards the site where the great Buddha was lying on his deathbed, where the great event was taking place, and where the savior of an age was passing into eternity.

At this time, Siddhartha thought a great deal about the dying sage whose voice had stirred thousands, whose voice he once heard, whose holy countenance he once gazed with awe. He lovingly thought of the Buddha, passionately remembered Buddha's path to salvation, and while smiling, fondly recalled the words he once talked to the Illustrious One when he was still a young man. It seemed to him that at the time, his words were quite arrogant but somewhat precocious.

For a long time, he knew that he was not separated from Gotama even though he could not accept the Illustrious One's teachings back then. No, a true seeker could not accept any teachings if he sincerely wished to find something, otherwise. However, true seekers who found the truth could agree with every path and could agree with every goal. Nothing could separate true seekers who found the truth from thousands of thousands of those who lived in eternity and breathed the Divine.

One day, when so many people were making a pilgrimage to the dying Buddha, Kamala, who was once the most beautiful courtesan, was also on her way. She had long retired from her previous way of life, had presented her pleasure garden to Gotama's monks, and had taken refuge in his teachings. She had also become one of the benefactresses who often gave alms to the poor and attached to the pilgrims.

On hearing of Gotama's approaching death, she wore simple clothes and set off on foot together with her son. When they reached the river bank, the boy became tired. He wanted to go back home so that he could eat and rest. He became more often sulky and tearful. Kamala had to frequently rest with him. As usual, he was used to match his will against her will. She had to feed him, comfort him, and scold him. He could not understand why his mother had to make this weary, miserable pilgrimage to an unknown place and to a strange man who was holy and was dying. Let the holy man die. What did it matter to him?

When this group of pilgrims was not far from the Vasudeva's ferry, the little Siddhartha told his mother that he wanted to rest. Kamala, herself, was also tired, so they both stopped for a little break. While the boy ate a banana, she crouched down on the ground to rest with her eyes hanging half-closed.

Suddenly, however, she uttered a cry of pain. While being startled, the boy looked at his mother and saw her face turn white as a result of horror. From under her clothes, a small black snake, which just bit her, crawled away.

Both the mother and the son, while holding each other's hand, ran on quickly in order to reach out to people. When they were near the ferry, Kamala collapsed and could not go any farther. The boy cried out for help, but in the meantime, he kissed and embraced his mother. She also joined in his loud cries until the sounds of their mourning voices reached Vasudeva who stood by the ferry. In a hurry, Vasudeva ran to them, quickly took the woman in his arms, and carried her to the boat. The boy joined Vasudeva, and they soon arrived at the hut where Siddhartha was standing by the hearth and was just lighting a fire. Siddhartha looked up, and for the first time, he saw the boy's face that strangely but vehemently reminded him of something. He then saw Kamala whom he recognized immediately, even though she lay unconscious in Vasudeva's arms. Now, he knew that the boy was his son whose face ardently reminded him of something. His heart beat quickly.

Kamala's wound was washed and was blotted dry, but it was already black. Her entire body was also already swollen. A restorative was given to her, and her consciousness returned. She was lying on Siddhartha's bed in the hut, and Siddhartha, whom she had once loved very much, was bending over to gaze at her. She thought she was dreaming. With a sweet, gentle smile, she fixed her eyes on her lover's face. Gradually, she realized her condition, remembered the bite, and called anxiously for her son.

"Do not worry," whispered Siddhartha, "he is here."

Kamala passionately gazed into Siddhartha' eyes, but she found it very difficult to speak because of the poison in her system.

"You have grown old, my dear," spoke Kamala with a heavy tongue. "You have become gray, but you are like the young Samana who once came to me in my garden, without clothes and with dusty feet. You now look much more like that young Samana than the old Siddhartha who left Kamaswami and me. Your eyes are like those of the young Samana as well, Siddhartha. Ah, I have also grown old, grown old. Did you recognize me?"

Siddhartha smiled, "I recognized you immediately, Kamala, my dear."

Kamala indicated her son and tried to speak as her voice grew croakier, "Did you recognize him, too? He is your son."

Her eyes wandered and closed. The boy began to cry. Siddhartha put him on his knees, let him weep, and stroked his hair. Looking at the child's face, he recalled a Brahmin prayer that he once learned when he himself was a small child. In a singing voice, he slowly began to recite it. Warmhearted prayer words came back to him from the past and from his childhood. The child became quiet as the father recited the prayer. Once in a short while, he sobbed a little and then fell asleep. Siddhartha put him on Vasudeva's bed. Vasudeva stood by the hearth cooking rice, but he never stopped keeping his eyes on Siddhartha. Siddhartha looked at Vasudeva and saw Vasudeva smiling with him.

"She is dying," said Siddhartha softly.

Vasudeva nodded while the firelight from the hearth was reflected on his kind face.

Kamala again regained her consciousness, but the unbearable pain was clearly painted on her face.

Siddhartha read the heart-rending pain in her mouth and on her pallid face. He read it quietly, attentively, tenderly, and affectionately—it seemed as if through their heart connection, he tried to share the pain with her. Kamala was well aware that Siddhartha endeavored to share her pain. Her glance wandered to seek his eyes.

While looking at the Siddhartha's eyes, Kamala said, "Now, I see that your eyes have also changed. They are quite different. How do I recognize that you are still Siddhartha? You are Siddhartha, but you are not like him."

Siddhartha did not utter a word. Silently, he gazed into her eyes.

"Have you attained it?" asked Kamala. "Have you found peace?"

Siddhartha smiled and placed his hand on hers.

"Yes," said Kamala, "I see it. I will also find peace."

"You have found it. You have found it. You have found it," Siddhartha said with a compassionate voice, which gradually grew into almost silence as tears were choking him.

Kamala looked at Siddhartha steadily. It was her intention to make a pilgrimage to Gotama, to see the face of the Illustrious One, and to obtain some of his peace, but instead, she found Siddhartha. It was good, just as equally good, if she saw Gotama. She wanted to tell Siddhartha about what her intention was and about what was in mind, but her tongue no longer obeyed her will. Silently, she looked at him, and he saw the life fade away from her eyes. When the last pain that had filled her eyes moved past her vision and when the last shudder that had swept through her entire body disappeared into a sublime stillness, his fingers closed her eyelids.

Siddhartha sat there a long time looking at her dead face. For a long time, he looked at her mouth, her old tired mouth, and looked at her shrunken lips. He recalled how once, in the spring of his life, he compared her lips with a freshly cut fig. For a long time, he looked intently at her pale face and at her tired wrinkles. He came to realize that his own face had been just like hers—it was just as white and as dead. At this same moment, he saw his face and hers become young again, brightened with red lips and with ardent eyes. He was overwhelmed with a feeling of the present and of the contemporary existence. In this hour, he had an intense feeling. More than ever before, he deeply felt the indestructibility of every life and the eternity of every moment.

When Siddhartha rose, Vasudeva had already prepared some rice for him, but Siddhartha did not feel like eating it. In the stable where the goat was, the two old men straightened out some straw for themselves. Vasudeva lay down, but Siddhartha went outside. He sat in front of the hut all night, listened to the river, and travelled back to the past. He let his heart be affected and encompassed by all periods of his life. From time to time, he rose and walked to the door of the hut. He carefully listened to make sure that the boy was sleeping.

Early in the morning, before the sun was yet visible, Vasudeva came out of the stable and walked up to his friend.

"You have not slept," said Vasudeva calmly.

"No, Vasudeva. I sat here and listened to the river," replied Siddhartha serenely. "It has told me a great deal. It has filled me with many great thoughts—thoughts of unity."

"You have suffered, Siddhartha, but I see that sadness has still not entered your heart," said Vasudeva placidly.

"No, my dear friend, why should I be sad?" answered Siddhartha composedly. "I, who was rich and happy, have now become richer and happier. I have been given a gift, and that is my son—my own son, my very own."

"I also welcome your son. But now, Siddhartha, let us go to work," urged Vasudeva, "There is much to be done. Kamala died on the same bed where my wife died. We shall have to build Kamala's funeral pyre on the very same hill where I once built my wife's funeral pyre."

While the boy was still sleeping, they built the funeral pyre.

Remark: The six roots of sensations that Siddhartha deadened during his ardent Samana years became quite awakened when he lived his material life. Once again, the six roots of sensations that he deadened during his blissful years living with Vasudeva became utterly awakened when he met Kamala and his son at the ferry . . .

By suffering from the death of Kamala, Siddhartha now deeply realized what the feeling of losing a loved one was like. It was not a simple pain, but it was rather the desperation. It was not a simple change, but it was rather the emptiness. These desperation and emptiness offer the evidences of how emotional attachments make sentient beings suffer and of why sentient beings always struggle to cope with the ephemeral nature of life.

CHAPTER 10

THE SON

Frightening and weeping, the boy attended his mother's burial. Frightening and disheartening, the boy listened to Siddhartha greeting him as his son and making him feel welcome in Vasudeva's hut. For days on end, with a pale face, the boy sat on the hill of the dead, stared off into the distance, locked his heart, fought off his saddened feelings, and strove against his fate.

Siddhartha treated his son with consideration and left his son alone because he respected the grief of his son. He understood that his son did not know him and that his son could not love him like the father. Slowly, he saw and realized that the eleven-year-old child was a spoilt mama's boy and had been brought up in the habits of the rich. The boy was accustomed to eating fine food, sleeping on a soft bed, and commanding servants. He also understood that the grief-stricken, spoiled boy could not suddenly be content in a strange and poor place, so he did not have the heart to press the boy into accepting anything. He helped the boy a great deal and always saved the best morsels for the boy. He hoped that slowly, he could win the boy over by being friendly, being kind, and by being patient.

Siddhartha had considered himself richer and happier when the boy had come to him. However, as time passed, the boy remained unfriendly to his father, still felt sulky, still wanted to talk to nobody, and still wished to be with neither Vasudeva nor him. When the boy proved arrogant and defiant, when the boy refused to work, when the boy showed no respect for the old people, when the boy robbed Vasudeva's fruit trees, and when the boy provoked his father, he began to realize that his son brought him no happiness and no peace. He now became conscious that only sorrow and trouble had come to him with his son. But, he loved the boy, so he preferred the sorrow and trouble with the boy rather than the happiness and peace without the boy.

Since young Siddhartha was in the hut, the old men began to split up the work. Vasudeva had taken over all the work on the ferry while Siddhartha, in order to be with his son, had handled all the work in the hut and on the field.

For many months, Siddhartha patiently waited in hope. He hoped that his son would come to understand him, that his son would accept his love, and that his son would perhaps love him in return. Also during those same many months, Vasudeva observed the situation, but unlike Siddhartha, he patiently waited in silence instead of in hope. One day, when young Siddhartha was distressing his father with a spiteful tone of defiance and a bad temper, he broke both rice bowls.

Vasudeva took his friend aside in the evening and talked to him.

"Forgive me," said Vasudeva, "I am speaking to you as if you are my friend. I can see that you are worried and unhappy. Your son, my dear friend, is troubling you and troubling me. The young bird is accustomed to a different life and is accustomed to a different nest. He did not give up riches, did not run away from the town with a feeling of nausea, and did not abandon materials with a feeling of disgust as you did. On the contrary, he has had to leave all those things against his will. I have asked the river, my friend. I have asked it many times, and it laughs every time. It laughs at me, and it laughs at you. It shakes itself with laughter at our folly. Water will go to water, and youth will go to youth. Your son will never be happy in this place. You should ask the river and listen to what it says!"

Anxiously, Siddhartha looked at Vasudeva's kind face on which there were many good-natured wrinkles.

"How can I part from my son?" said Siddhartha softly. "Give me some time, my dear friend. I am fighting for him. I am trying to reach his heart. I will win him with love and patience. The river will also talk to my son some day. He will also be called."

Vasudeva's smile became warmer. "Oh yes," said Vasudeva. "He will also be called because he also belongs to the everlasting life. But do you and I know to what he will be called, to which path he will take, into which judgment will his deeds bring, and from what sorrows he will suffer? His sorrows will not be slight because his heart is proud and hard. He will probably suffer much, make many mistakes, commit many sins, and do much injustice. Tell me, my friend, are you educating your son? Is he obedient to you? Do you strike him or punish him?"

"No, Vasudeva," Siddhartha distressingly shook his head, "I do not do anything of those things."

"I knew it," said Vasudeva firmly. "You are not strict with him, and you do not punish him. You do not command him because you know that gentleness is stronger than severity; you know that water is stronger than rocks; and you know that love is stronger than force. Very good, I praise you. But is it not perhaps a mistake on your part that you are not strict with him and do not punish him? Do you not chain him to your love? Do you not shame him daily with your goodness and with your patience? Do you not make it more difficult for him to deal with an awkward situation? Do you not compel this arrogant, spoiled boy to live in a hut with two old banana eaters to whom even rice is a delicacy, whose thoughts are not on the same frequency as his, whose hearts are old and quiet, and whose heartbeats have different patterns from his? Is the boy not constrained and punished by all these things?"

Siddhartha looked down to the ground in complete perplexity. "What do you think I should do?" asked Siddhartha softly.

Vasudeva said, "Take him into the town. Take him to his mother's house. There will still be servants there. Give him to them. And if they are no longer there, take him to a teacher. It is not just for the sake of education, but it is for him to meet other boys and other girls so that he can be in the world to which he belongs. Have you ever thought about it?"

"You can see into my heart," said Siddhartha sadly. "Yes, I have often thought about it. But how will he who is so hard-hearted go on in this world? Will he not consider himself superior? Will he not lose himself in pleasure and power? Will he not repeat all his father's mistakes? And will he not perhaps be quite lost in Samsara?"

Vasudeva smiled again. He gently touched Siddhartha's arm and said, "Ask the river about it, my friend! Listen to its laughter when it talks to you! Do you really think that you committed follies in order to spare your son? Can you protect your son from Samsara? How? How do you protect him from Samsara? Through instructions? Through prayers? Through exhortations? My dear friend, have you forgotten the instructive story about Siddhartha, a Brahman's son, which you once told me? Who protected Siddhartha, the Samana, from Samsara, from sins, from greed, and from follies? Could his father's piety, his teachers' exhortations, his own knowledge, and his own seeking protect him? Could his father stop him from becoming a Samana? Which teacher could prevent him from living his own life, from soiling himself with life, from loading himself with sins, from swallowing the bitter drink, and from finding his own path? Who could prevent Siddhartha from experiencing unpleasant moments, painful situations, and embarrassing feelings? My dear friend, do you really think that somebody out there might perhaps be spared from this path? Do you really think that somebody out there is perhaps your little son, just because you would like to see him being spared from sorrows, from pain, and from disillusionment? But, my dear friend, even if you were willing to die ten times for him, you would still not alter his destiny in the slightest."

Never had Vasudeva talked this much before. Siddhartha thanked him in a friendly fashion, went to the hut with his heart full of troubles, and could not fall asleep. Vasudeva had not said anything that Siddhartha had not already thought of them and known about them himself. But stronger than his knowledge was his love for the boy, his devotion to the boy, and his fear of losing the boy. Had he ever lost his heart to anyone so completely? Had he ever loved anyone so deeply, so blindly, so painfully, so hopelessly, and yet so happily?

Siddhartha could not take Vasudeva's advice. He could not give up his son. He allowed the boy to order him and allowed the boy to be disrespectful to him. He continued to be silent and continued to wait. Every day, he exerted himself to the utmost to recommence the mute battle of friendliness and of patience.

Vasudeva was also silent and waited in friendliness, in compassion, and in forbearance. They both were the masters of patience.

One day, when the boy's face reminded Siddhartha of Kamala, he suddenly remembered something that she once told him, "You cannot love." She said to him, and he agreed with her. He compared himself with a star and compared other people with falling leaves. Nonetheless, he did feel some kind of reproach in her words. It was true that he never fully lost himself in another person to such an extent that he forgot himself. He also never loved anyone to such an extent that he submitted himself to follies. He was never capable of loving another person more than loving himself. It seemed to him that the incapability of committing the follies of love was the biggest difference between him and the ordinary people. Now, since he had known that he had a son of his own, he had become completely like all ordinary people who plunged themselves into sorrows because of loving too much. He was madly in love and became a fool because of love. Now, belatedly, he experienced the strongest yet strangest passion for the first time ever in his life. He suffered tremendously because of this passion, but at the same time, it uplifted his soul, renewed his soul, and made his soul richer in some way.

He, indeed, felt that this love, this blind love for his son, was a very human passion. This human passion was nothing but Samsara—a troubled deep spring filled with wind-rippled waves. By the same token, he felt that it was not worthless—it was necessary, and it came from his own nature. This human passion, this Samsara, and these follies of love all had to be experienced.

In the meantime, the boy let his father commit the follies, let his father strive, let his father bear all affronts, and let his father be humbled by his moods. To the boy, this father had nothing that could attract him and had nothing that could threaten him. This father was a good man, a kind man, a gentle man, perhaps a pious man, and perhaps a holy man, but none of these qualities could win over the boy. This father, who always kept him in the wretched hut, bored him. When the father answered his rudeness with a smile, answered his insult with friendliness, and answered his naughtiness with a kindness, he became so annoyed and could not control his temper. The way the father responded to his actions was the most hateful cunning of the old fox. He would much prefer his father to threaten him and to ill-treat him.

One day, the young Siddhartha said what was in his mind and openly turned against his father. Siddhartha told the boy to gather some twigs, but he did not leave the hut. He stood up, in defiance and anger, stamped his feet on the floor, clenched his fists, and ruthlessly threw his hatred and contempt into his father's face.

"Bring your own twigs!" the boy foamed at the mouth as he shouted, "I am not your servant. I know that you do not beat me. You dare not! I, however, know that you will continually punish me and will make me feel small with your piety, your kindness, and your compassion. You want me to become like you, so pious, so gentle, and so wise. But just to spite you, I would rather become a thief, turn into a murderer, and go to hell rather than be like you! I hate you. You are not my father even though you were my mother's lover many dozen times!"

Full of rage and misery, the boy found an outlet in a stream full of wild and angry words and threw them straight into his father's face. He then ran away and did not return until late in the evening.

The following morning, the boy disappeared. A small two-colored basket, made of bast, that the ferrymen used to keep the copper and silver coins which they received as payments for their services was also disappeared. The boat was disappeared as well. Siddhartha saw the empty boat on the other side of the bank. It turned out that the boy had run away.

"I must follow him," said Siddhartha who had been in great distress because of the boy's harsh words yesterday. "A child like him cannot go through the forest alone. He will come across some harm. We must make a raft, Vasudeva, in order to get to the other side of the river."

"We will make a raft," said Vasudeva, "in order to fetch our boat that the boy took away. However, let him go, my friend. He is not a child anymore. He knows how to look after himself. He is finding his way back to the town, and he is making the right decision for himself. Do not forget that he is doing what you, yourself, neglected to do. He is looking after himself. He is going his own way. Oh, Siddhartha, I can see you are suffering. You suffer the pain that other people could laugh at you and that you will soon laugh at yourself, too."

Siddhartha did not reply. He already held the hatchet in his hands and began to build a raft from bamboo. Vasudeva helped him to bind the canes together with grass rope. They then tried to sail the raft across the river, but it was drifting far down the stream, opposite to the direction where they wanted to go. However, they eventually managed to direct it back up the stream and then head to the other bank.

"Why have you brought the hatchet with you?" asked Siddhartha.

Vasudeva said, "It is possible that the oar of our boat may already be lost."

Siddhartha, however, knew what his friend was thinking Vasudeva probably believed that the boy already threw the oar away or broke it out of revenge or hid it somewhere in order to prevent the two old men from following him. And indeed, the oar was no longer in the boat.

Vasudeva pointed at the bottom of the boat and smiled to his friend as if he wanted to say, "Do you not see what your son wishes to say? Do you not see that he does not wish to be followed?" He, however, did not say what he had in mind and started to make a new oar. Without uttering a word, Siddhartha took leave of his friend to look for the boy, and Vasudeva did not hinder him.

Siddhartha had been in the forest for a long time before he realized that his search was useless. Regardless of whichever one of two scenarios, he was not going to find the boy. First, if the boy had left the wood for a long time ago, he would have already reached the town. Second, if he still had been on the way, he would have hidden from the pursuer. When he reflected further, he found that he was no longer worried about his son. Deep down inside, he knew that the boy had neither come across harm nor stumbled upon danger in the forest. Nevertheless, he went on steadily with no hesitation. He no longer wished to save the boy, but with a heartfelt desire, he hoped to see the boy again. He kept on walking up to the outskirt of the town.

When he reached the wide road near the town, he stood still at the entrance to the beautiful pleasure garden that was once belonged to Kamala. This was also the entrance where he saw her in a sedan chair for the first time. The past rose before his eyes. Once again, he saw himself standing there—a young Samana in torn clothes, with bristly beard, and with dusty hair. Siddhartha stood there a long time and looked through the open gate into the garden where he saw the monks sauntering beneath the beautiful trees.

While standing at the entrance for a long time, he was thinking about the past, seeing snapshots in his youth, and listening to the stories of his life. He stood there for a long time gazing at the monks, but he only saw the young Samana and Kamala walking together beneath the tall trees. Clearly, he saw himself being intimately attended by Kamala and receiving her first kiss. When he looked back on his Samana days, he saw how arrogant and how contemptuous he was. He also saw how proud and how eager he was when he began his worldly life. When he saw Kamaswami, the servants, the banquets, the dice players, and the musicians, he also saw Kamala's songbird in its small golden cage. He lived every single stage of his life all over again—breathed the Samsara, became old, felt worn out, experienced nausea, desired to take his own life, and finally heard the holy Om.

After he stood for a long time at the entrance to the beautiful pleasure garden, he realized that the desire that had driven him to this place was foolish.

He also realized that he could not help his son and could not force himself on the boy. He felt that his deep love for the runaway boy was like a wound, but at the same time, he felt that this wound in his heart was not intended to worsen and was supposed to heal.

Because the wound did not heal during this hour, he was still sad. Instead of the goal that brought him here to seek the boy, there was only the emptiness left inside of him. Sadly, he sat down. He felt as if something died in his heart. He saw no more happiness and no more goals in his life. He sat there feeling depressed and waiting, but he allowed himself to listen to his thoughts. This was what he had learned from the river—to wait, to be patient, and to listen. In the dusty road, he sat to listen, listened to his heart that beat wearily and sadly, and waited for a voice. He crouched there and listened for many hours, but he saw no more visions. He sank into emptiness and let him keep sinking without seeing a way out. And when he felt the wound smarting, he soundlessly pronounced the word Om and filled himself with it.

The monks in the garden saw him. As he sat down at the entrance and crouched there for many hours, the dust on the road was collected on his gray hair. One of the monks came towards him and placed two bananas in front of him, but he did not see the monk.

A warm hand touched Siddhartha's shoulder and awakened him from his trance. He recognized this gentle, timid touch and recovered. He rose and greeted Vasudeva who had been following him. When he saw Vasudeva's kind face, gazed at his little laughter wrinkles, and looked into Vasudeva's bright eyes, he smiled as well.

Siddhartha now saw two bananas lying near him. He picked them up, gave one to Vasudeva, and ate the other one. He then silently walked through the wood with Vasudeva and returned to the ferry. Neither of them spoke a word of what just happened. Neither of them mentioned the boy's name, talked about the boy's flight, and brought up the wound imposed by the boy.

Siddhartha went to his bed in the hut. When Vasudeva went to the bed some time later to offer him a bowl of coconut milk, he found Siddhartha already asleep.

Remark: No one should impose his thoughts and his way of life on others, especially on his loved ones. Everyone has to experience oneself.

CHAPTER 11

OM

The wound continued to smart Siddhartha for a long time. He took many travelers who had sons or daughters with them across the river. He could not look at any them without envying them and without whispering to himself, "So many people possess this very great happiness. Why can I not? Even wicked people, thieves, and robbers have children, love their children, and are loved by their children," released a sigh the weary man, "except me." So childishly and so illogically, he reasoned. So much had he become like the ordinary people.

He now regarded people differently from how he did before. He no longer assumed that he was very clever and no longer believed that he was supposed to feel very proud of himself; thus, he was much warmer, more curious, and more sympathetic. Now, when he took the usual kind of travelers like businessmen, soldiers, and women across, they no longer seemed to be alien to him as they once were. He neither understood nor shared their thoughts and views, but he felt the urges to live and the desires to love as much as they did. Although he had reached a high level of self-discipline and had borne his last wound well, he now felt as if all ordinary people were his brothers and his sisters. Their vanities, their desires, and their trivialities no longer seemed to be absurd to him. Now, they were becoming more understandable; becoming more lovable; and becoming even more worthy of respect. There was the blind love of a mother for her child. There was the blind love and the foolish pride of a fond father for his only son. There were the blind striving and the absurd eagerness of a young, vain woman for beautification and for the admiration of men. All these urges, which were foolish yet tremendously strong, and all these desires, which were passionate yet extremely vital, no longer seemed to be trivial to Siddhartha.

For the sakes of these urges and desires, he saw people living and doing great things. He also saw people travelling everywhere, conducting wars, creating tremendous suffering, and enduring immense hardship. And this was why he loved them. He now realized that life, vitality, and the indestructible Brahmin were in all of their desires and needs. These people were worthy of love and were worthy of admiration in their blind loyalty, in their strength, and in their tenacity. They had everything that the sages and thinkers had with the exception of one small thing, one tiny little thing, that was the consciousness of the unity of all living things. Many times, Siddhartha even doubted whether the knowledge of unity or the thought of unity was of such great value or of importance or not. Again and again, he even wondered whether the knowledge of unity or the thought of unity was perhaps the childish, self-flattery of thinkers, who were probably thinking children, or not. The worldly men who were equal to the thinkers in all aspects often appeared to be far more superior than the thinkers in many ways were when needed. Exactly like animals in case of necessity, they usually seemed to be far more superior compared to human beings in their tenacious undeviating actions.

Within the Siddhartha's soul, there slowly grew and ripened the knowledge of what wisdom really was and the goal of how long his seeking was. It was nothing but the preparation of the soul, the capacity, the secret art of thinking, the feeling, and the breathing thoughts about unity at every moment of life. These thoughts—the harmony of thoughts, the eternal perfection of the world at all times, and the unity of all living things—slowly became matured within him, but they were clearly reflected in Vasudeva's old childlike face.

The wound, however, still smarted. Yearningly and bitterly, Siddhartha thought about his son. He continued to nurture his love and feelings of tenderness for the boy. He let the pain gnaw at him and committed all the follies of love. The flame within him did not extinguish itself.

One day, when the wound was smarting terribly, Siddhartha rowed across the river whilst his soul was consumed with longing. He got out of the boat with the purpose of going to the town to seek his son. The river flowed softly and gently. Now, it was in the dry season, but the voice of the river rang out strangely. Apparently, it was laughing. Distinctly, it was laughing! Clearly, it was laughing. Merrily and clearly, it was laughing at the old, doting ferryman.

Siddhartha stood still but then bent over the water in order to hear the voice better. He saw his face reflected in the quietly moving water, and there was something in the reflection that reminded him of someone whom he had long forgotten. As his face was reflected in the water, he remembered. His face resembled the face of another person whom he had once known, loved, and even feared. His face resembled the face of his father, the Brahmin. He remembered, as a youth, how he had compelled his father to let him go and join the ascetics; how he had taken leave of his parents; how he had kept on going; and how he had never once returned. Did his father not suffer the same pain that he was now suffering because of his son? Did his father not die alone long ago without seeing his only son again? Did he not expect the exact same fate that his father had? Was it not a comedy, a strange situation, and a stupid story? Was this recurrence, this course of all events in a circle of fate?

The river laughed out loud. Yes, that was how things happened in life. Everything that was not suffered to the end in order to finally conclude occurred again. The same sorrows were undergone all over again. Siddhartha then climbed back into the boat and rowed toward the hut. On the way, he was thinking of his father and was thinking of his son while the river was still laughing at him for being in conflict with himself. Even standing on the verge of despair, he no less inclined to laugh aloud at himself and at the whole world. The wound still smarted, but he still rebelled against his fate. There were still no serenity and still no conquest of his suffering. Yet, he was hopeful. When he returned to the hut, he was filled with an unconquerable desire to confess to Vasudeva and to disclose everything to him. He wanted to tell the ferryman who knew the art of listening to everything.

Vasudeva sat in the hut weaving a basket. He no longer worked at the ferryboat. His eyes were growing weak, and so were his arms and his hands. He was growing old, but the radiant look and the serene well-being on his face remained unchanged.

Siddhartha sat down beside the old man and slowly began to speak. He now told Vasudeva everything that he had never mentioned before. He told Vasudeva how anxiously he went to the town last time, how painfully his wound hurt him, how envy he felt at the sight of happy fathers, how mindful he was of the knowledge of the folly of such feelings, and how hopelessly he struggled with himself.

He finally mentioned everything to Vasudeva. He could finally disclose everything to Vasudeva. Even the most painful feelings, he was able to tell Vasudeva everything. He showed Vasudeva his wound and told Vasudeva about his flight earlier today. He told Vasudeva how he rowed across the river with the intention of wandering into the town and how the river laughed at him.

As he went on speaking, and as Vasudeva listened to him with a serene face, more than ever before, Siddhartha was keenly aware of Vasudeva's attentiveness. He felt that his troubles, his anxieties, and his secret hopes flowed across him to Vasudeva and then returned to him. Disclosing his wound to this listener was not any different from letting the wound bath in the river until it became cool and became one with the river.

As Siddhartha went on talking and confessing, he felt more and more that this listener was no longer Vasudeva and no longer a man who was listening to him. He felt that this motionless listener was absorbing his confession as a tree absorbed the rain. He felt that this motionless man, indeed, was the river himself, was God himself, and was the eternity himself. As Siddhartha stopped thinking about himself and about his wound, the recognition of the change in Vasudeva possessed him. The more he realized the change in Vasudeva, the less strange Vasudeva became to him, and the more did he recognize that everything existed in its own natural being. Long ago, Vasudeva had almost always been like that, but Siddhartha did not quite recognize who Vasudeva was. Indeed, Siddhartha, himself, was hardly different from Vasudeva. He felt that he now regarded Vasudeva exactly as the people regarded the gods, but this high regard could not last long. Inwardly, he began to take leave of Vasudeva even though in the mean time, he went on talking.

When Siddhartha finished talking, Vasudeva directed his somewhat weakened glance at Siddhartha. Although Vasudeva did not utter a word, his face silently radiated not only love and serenity but also knowledge and wisdom. He then took Siddhartha's hand, led Siddhartha to the seat on the river bank, sat down beside Siddhartha, and smiled to the river.

"You have heard it laugh," said Vasudeva, "but you have not heard everything. Let us now listen together. You will hear it a lot more."

They both listened. The many-voiced song of the river echoed softly. Siddhartha looked into the river and saw many pictures in the flowing water. He saw his father, who was lonely, mourning for his only son. He saw himself, who was also lonely, grieving over the bonds of longing for his own faraway son. He saw his son, the young Siddhartha, who was also lonely, but unlike his father and him, the boy eagerly advanced along the burning path of life that was filled with passions and desires. All three of them—the father, the old Siddhartha, and the young Siddhartha—concentrated on their own goal. All three of them were obsessed by their own goal and thus suffered their own miseries. The river's voice was sorrowful. It sang with yearning and with sadness, but it slowly flowed towards its goal.

"Do you hear, my friend?" asked Vasudeva's mute glance.

"Yes, I do," muttered Siddhartha with a nod.

"Keep listening to it. Listen to it better!" murmured Vasudeva.

Siddhartha tried to listen better. The picture of his father, the picture of his own, and the picture of his son all flowed into each other. The picture of Kamala also appeared and flowed on. The picture of Govinda and the pictures of many others also merged and passed. Each one of them was a part of the river; hence, the voice of the river reflected the goals of all of them. They all yearned for something, desired for something, and thus inevitably suffered something. For this reason, the river's voice was full of longing, full of craving, full of smarting woes, and full of insatiable desires. The river flowed on towards its goal.

Siddhartha saw the river, which was made up of himself, of his relatives, and of all people he had ever seen in his life, hasten. All the waves and water hastened, suffered, and flowed towards their goals—their many goals. They flowed to the fields, to the waterfalls, to the currents, and into the oceans. After they reached all goals, they then proceeded to new ones.

Water changed to vapor and rose. Vapor then condensed into liquid and came down to become rain. Water became a spring, a brook, or a river that flowed anew and changed anew. For these reasons, the yearning voice of the water also changed anew. It still echoed sorrowfully and searchingly, but other voices now accompanied it—voices of pleasure, voices of sorrow, voices of good, voices of evil, voices of laughter, and voices of lamentation. Hundreds of other voices and thousands of other voices joined in together.

Siddhartha listened. Now, he intently listened and was utterly absorbed by the river. With a quiet heart and an empty soul, he took in everything. He felt that he had now completely learned the art of listening. He often heard all these voices before, all these numerous muddled voices from the river, but today, they sounded different. Now, he could no longer distinguish differences among these numerous voices. He could no longer differentiate the merry voice from the weeping voice or the childish voice from the full-fledged voice.

They all belonged to each other—the lament of those who yearned, the laughter of those who became wise, the cry of those who suffered, the indignation of those who experienced injustice, and the groan of those who were dying. They were all interwoven, interlocked, and entwined with each other in a thousand ways. And all the voices, all the goals, all the yearnings, all the sorrows, all the pleasures, all the good, and all the evils blended into each other to form the world. Together, it was the stream of events and was the music of life.

When Siddhartha attentively listened to this river, listened to this thousand-voiced song, he listened to neither the sorrow nor the laughter. When he bound his soul to no particular voice and allowed all voices to absorb into his *Self*, he heard them all—the whole, the unity. Now, the great song of a thousand voices consisted only of one word—Om, perfection.

"Do you hear," asked Vasudeva's glance once again.

Vasudeva's smile was radiant. His smile hovered brightly in all the wrinkles of his old face, just as the Om hovered over all the voices of the river. His smile was radiant as he looked at his friend, Siddhartha.

Now, the same smile appeared on Siddhartha's face. His wound was healing; his pain was dispersing; and his *Self* was merging into unity.

From that very hour, Siddhartha ceased to fight against his destiny. Shone on his face was the serenity of knowledge. It was the knowledge of the one who no longer confronted with conflicts of desires and had found salvation. It was the knowledge of the one who was in harmony with the stream of events, was in harmony with the stream of life, was filled with sympathy, and was filled with compassion. It was also the knowledge of the one who surrendered himself to the stream of life and submitted himself to the unity of all things.

As Vasudeva rose from the seat on the river bank and looked into the Siddhartha's eyes, he saw the serenity of the knowledge shining in those eyes. He gently touched Siddhartha's shoulder in his usual kind, protective way and said, "I have been waiting for this hour, my friend. Now that it arrives. Let me go. I have been Vasudeva, the ferryman, for a long time. Now that it is over for me. Farewell hut! Farewell river! Farewell Siddhartha! Farewell all!"

Siddhartha bowed low before the departing man.

"I knew it," said Siddhartha softly. "Are you going into the woods?"

"Yes, I am going into the woods. I am going into the unity of all things," said Vasudeva, radiant.

And Vasudeva went away.

Siddhartha watched his friend.

With great joy and gravity, Siddhartha watched him go. His steps were full of peace; his radiant face was glowing; and his form was full of light.

Remark: Siddhartha's fifth awakening—Developing an inner atmosphere of respect where love and compassion could grow and thrive was Siddhartha's fifth awakening. After experiencing intolerable pain, he became awakened that nothing in life was trivial and that every lesson learned had its own price.

CHAPTER 12

GOVINDA

One time, Govinda and a few other monks spent a rest period in the pleasure grove which Kamala, the courtesan, once presented it to the followers of Gotama. He heard people talking of an old ferryman who lived a day's journey away by the river and regarded as a sage by many.

When Govinda moved on to beg for alms, he chose the path to the ferry because he was eager to see the old ferryman. Although he always followed the rules and always received high respect from the younger monks for his age and modesty, the restlessness and the seeking in his heart remained unsettled.

He arrived at the river bank and asked the old ferryman to take him across the river. When they climbed out of the boat on the other side, he said to the old ferryman, "You show much kindness to the monks and pilgrims. You have taken many of us across. Are you not also a seeker of the right path?"

There was a smile in Siddhartha's old eyes as he said, "Do you call yourself a seeker, O venerable one, while you are already advanced in years and wear the robe of Gotama's monks?"

"I am, indeed, old," said Govinda, "but I have never ceased seeking. I will never cease seeking. That seems to be my destiny. It seems to me that you had also sought before. Could you tell me a little about it, my friend?"

Siddhartha said, "What would be of value that I could tell you, O venerable one, except that you perhaps seek too much? As a result of your seeking too much, you cannot find what you seek."

"How is that?" asked Govinda.

"When someone is seeking," said Siddhartha, "it happens quite easily that he only sees the thing that he is seeking. He is unable to find anything else and unable to absorb anything else because he is only thinking of the thing he is seeking. Because he has a goal, and because he is obsessed with his goal, he is incapable of seeing anything else. Seeking means having a goal while finding means being free or being receptive or having no goal. You, O worthy one, are perhaps, indeed, a seeker because while striving towards your goal, you did not see many things that were under your nose."

"I do not yet quite understand," said Govinda, "How do you mean?"

Siddhartha said, "Once, O worthy one, many years ago, you came to this river and found a man sleeping here. You sat beside him to guard him while he slept, but you did not recognize who the sleeping man was, Govinda."

Astonished like one bewitched, the monk gazed at the old ferryman.

"Are you Siddhartha?" asked Govinda in a timid voice. "I did not recognize you this time, either. I am very pleased to see you again, Siddhartha, very pleased. You have changed very much, my friend. Have you become a ferryman now?"

Siddhartha warmly laughed out loud, "Yes, I have now become a ferryman. Many people have to change a great deal and have to wear all sorts of clothes. I am one of those, my friend. You are very welcome, Govinda, and I invite you to stay the night with me in my hut."

Govinda stayed the night in the hut and slept on the bed that once belonged to Vasudeva. Govinda asked the friend of his youth many questions, and Siddhartha had a great deal to tell him about his life.

On the following morning, when it was time for Govinda to depart, he talked to Siddhartha with some hesitation, "Before I go on my way, Siddhartha, I would like to ask you one more question. Do you uphold a doctrine, a belief, or a knowledge that helps you live and helps do the right things?"

Siddhartha said, "You have already known, my friend. Even as a young man, when we lived with the ascetics in the forest, I came to distrust not only doctrines but also teachers and turned my back on them. Even though, since that time, I had many teachers, I am still of the same turn of mind. A beautiful courtesan was my teacher for a long time. A rich merchant and a dice player were also my teachers. On one occasion, one of the Buddha's wandering monks was my teacher. He halted his pilgrimage to sit beside me for a long while when I fell asleep in the forest. I also learned something from him, and I am grateful to him, very grateful. However, among all teachers, I have learned the most from this river and from my predecessor, Vasudeva. He is, indeed, a simple man. He is not a thinker, but he realizes the most essential things as well as Gotama does. He is, in fact, a holy man, a saint."

Govinda said, "Siddhartha, it seems to me that you still like to jest a little. I believe you and know that you have not followed any teacher, but how could it be possible that even you, yourself, have no doctrine and no thought? How could you not discover certain thoughts or certain insights that help you live? It would give me great pleasure if you could tell me something about them."

Siddhartha said, "Yes, I have thoughts and insights here and there. Sometimes, for an hour or for a day, I become aware of the knowledge within me, just as one feels life in one's heart. Yes, I have a few thoughts, but it is difficult for me to tell you about them. However, here is one thought that has impressed me most, Govinda. Wisdom is not communicable. The wisdom which a wise man tries to communicate always sounds foolish."

"Are you jesting?" asked Govinda.

"No, I am telling you what I have discovered," said Siddhartha with a smile, "Knowledge can be communicated, but wisdom cannot. Everyone can find wisdom, can live with it, can strengthen by it, and can do wonders through it, but no one can pass it on to others or can teach it to others. I suspected this thought when I was still a youth, and it was this suspicion that drove me away from teachers."

Siddhartha paused for a little while and then continued, "There is another thought I have, Govinda, but perhaps, you will again think that it is a jest or folly. The thought is that in every truth, the opposite is equally true. For example, a truth can be expressed and can be enveloped in words only if it is one-sided. Everything that is thought and expressed in words is one-sided, only half the truth, because it lacks totality, completeness, and unity. When the Illustrious Buddha taught about the world, he had to divide it into Samsara and Nirvana, into illusion and truth, and into suffering and salvation. Otherwise, no one can do it. There is no other method for those who teach. However, the world that is within and around us is never one-sided. Never is a man or a deed wholly Samsara or wholly Nirvana. Never is a man wholly a saint or wholly a sinner. Everyone or everything appears to be wholly one way or the other because we suffer from the illusion that time is something real. Time is not real, Govinda. I have realized this time perception repeatedly. Now, if time is not real, then the dividing line that seems to lie between this material world and the eternity, between suffering and bliss, and between good and evil is also an illusion."

"How is that?" asked Govinda while puzzled.

"Listen, my friend!" explained Siddhartha, "I am a sinner, and you are also a sinner, but someday, the sinner will again be a Brahmin, will again attain Nirvana, and will again become a Buddha. Now, this 'someday' is just an illusion. It is only a comparison. The sinner is not on the way to a Buddha-like state. He is not evolving even though our thinking cannot conceive the situation. No, the truth of the matter is that the Buddhist nature already exists in the sinner, and the future already exists in the present. The hidden Buddhist nature must be recognized in the sinner, in everybody, in you, and in me as well. Govinda, my friend, the world is neither imperfect nor slowly evolving along a long path to perfection. No, it is perfect in every moment. Every sin already carries forgiveness within itself. All small children already carry latent forms of climacteric age within themselves. All suckling's already carry death within themselves; and within all dying people, there is already the eternal life. It is not possible for one person to see how far another person is on the way. The Buddha exists in the robber and in the dice player. On the contrary, the robber exists in the Brahmin. During deep meditation, we can dispel time to see the past, the present, and the future simultaneously. And when everything is good and everything is perfect, everything is then Brahmin."

"Therefore, it seems to me that everything that exists is good," said Siddhartha with a smile. "Death is as essential as life; sin is as essential as holiness; and wisdom is as essential as folly. Everything is necessary. Everything needs only my agreement, my assent, my love, and my understanding. Until then, all is well with me, and nothing can harm me. I have learned through my body and through my soul that it is necessary for me to sin, to sink into lustful desires, to strive for property, to experience nausea, and to plunge into the depths of despair in order to learn not to resist them. I have also learned through my body and through my soul that it is necessary for me to love the world, not to compare it with some kind of desired imaginary world or some kind of imaginary vision of perfection, to leave it as it is, and to be glad to belong to it. There it is, Govinda, it is the second thought which resides in my mind."

Siddhartha bent down, picked up a stone from the ground, and held it in his hand.

"This," said Siddhartha while gently juggling the stone back and forth between his fingers, "is a stone, and within a certain length of time, it will perhaps become soil. And from soil, it will become a plant, become an animal, or even become a man. If I had seen this stone in the past, I could perhaps have said, 'This stone is just a stone. It has no value. It belongs to the world of Maja, but because within the cycle of change, it becomes man and spirit that is also of importance.' That is what I might have thought in the past."

"But now," Siddhartha paused for a short while and then continued, "I think this stone is a stone. It is also an animal. It is also a god. It is also the Buddha. I do not respect it and do not love it because it is now one thing and then become something else in the future. However, I respect it and love it because it has already long been everything and will always be everything. I love it just because it is a stone and just because today, at this very moment, it is a stone. I see value and meaning in each one of its fine markings and in each one of its cavities. I also see its value and its meaning in the yellow, in the gray, in the hardness, and in the sound it makes when I knock on it in the dryness or in the dampness of its surface. There are stones that feel like oil or soap and that look like leaves or sand. Regardless, each one has its own feature and has its own way to worship Om. Each one is Brahmin. At the same time, it is very much like a stone, oily or soapy, but precisely, that just pleases me and makes me consider it to be wonderful and worthy of worship. However, I will say no more about it because words do not express thoughts very well. Thoughts always become a little different, a little distorted, and a little foolish immediately as they are expressed. In spite of this, it also pleases me because, perhaps, it seems right that what is of value or what is of wisdom to one man appears to be nonsense to another."

Govinda carefully listened in silence, but he hesitantly asked after a pause, "Why did you tell me about the stone?"

"I did so unintentionally," said Siddhartha, "but perhaps, what I just told you illustrates that I love the stone, and I love the river. I love all things at which we can look and from which we can learn. I can love a stone, Govinda. I can also love a tree or even a piece of bark. Yes, they are things, and man can love things. All men can love things, but no man can love words. Therefore, teachings are of no use to me because they have no hardness, no softness, no colors, no corners, no edges, no smell, and no taste. Teachings have nothing but words. Perhaps, this is the reason that prevents you from finding peace. Perhaps, there are too many words in teachings because even salvation, virtue, Samsara, and Nirvana are merely words, Govinda. Nirvana is not a thing or a place. It is only the word 'Nirvana'."

Govinda said, "Nirvana is not only the word, my friend. It is a thought."

Siddhartha continued, "It may be a thought, but my friend, I must confess that I do not differentiate very much between thoughts and words. Frankly, I do not attach great importance to thoughts, either. I attach more importance to things. For example, at this ferry, there was a man who was my predecessor and teacher. He was a holy man who, for many years, believed only in the river and nothing else. He noticed that the river's voice spoke to him, and he learned from it. It educated him and taught him. The river seemed like a god to him, and for many years, he did not know that every wind, every cloud, every bird, and every beetle are equally divine. They all know just as much as the river and can teach just as well as the esteemed river. However, when this holy man went off into the woods, he knew everything. He knew more than you and I even though he had no teacher and learned nothing from books. He just only believed in the river."

Govinda said, "But what you call 'thing', is it something real, something intrinsic? Is it not only the illusion of Maja, only the image, and only the appearance? Your stone, your tree, and your piece of bark, are they all real?"

"The fact that whether they are all real or unreal also does not trouble me much," said Siddhartha. "If they are all illusions, I am then also an illusion because theirs and mine are always of the same nature. This illusive nature, indeed, makes them so lovable and venerable. That is why I can love them."

"Here is another doctrine at which you will laugh, Govinda," smiled Siddhartha. "It seems to me that love is the most important thing in the world. It may be important to great thinkers to examine the world, to explain it, and to despise it. I, however, think it is only important to love the world, not to despise it, and it is only important to love each other, not to hate each other. We must be able to regard the world, all living beings, and all things with love, admiration, and respect."

"I understand that," said Govinda, "but this kind of love is just what the Illustrious One called illusion. He preached benevolence, generosity, forbearance, sympathy, and patience, but not love. He forbade us to bind ourselves to all kinds of earthly loves."

"I know that," said Siddhartha while smiling radiantly, "I know that, Govinda. Here we find ourselves within the maze of meanings and within the conflict of words because I do not deny that my words about love are apparently contradictory to Gotama's teachings. That is just why I distrust words so much, Govinda, because I know that this contradiction is only an illusion. I know that I am at one with Gotama. Indeed, how could he not know love? Although he recognizes all humanity's vanity and transitoriness, he loves humanity. He loves them so much that he has devoted a long life solely to help them and teach them. Also with this great teacher, similar to the thing that is of greater importance to me than the words, his deeds and his life are of greater importance to me than his teachings. The gestures of his hands and the peaceful look on his face are of greater importance to me than his opinions. Not in his speech or in his thought do I regard him as a great man, but it is in his deeds and in his life."

The two old men were silent for a long time. Then, as Govinda was preparing to go, he said, "I thank you, Siddhartha, for telling me something of your thoughts. Some of them are strange, so I cannot grasp them all immediately. However, I thank you, and I wish you many peaceful days."

Inwardly, Govinda, however, thought differently and mumbled to himself, "Siddhartha is a strange man. He expresses strange thoughts, and his ideas seem crazy. How different do the doctrines of the Illustrious One sound! The teachings of the Illustrious One are always clear, straightforward, and comprehensible. The words of the Illustrious One contain nothing strange, wild, or laughable. Siddhartha's hands and feet, his eyes, his brow, his breathing, his smile, his greeting, and his gait, however, affect me differently from his thoughts. Never, since the time the Illustrious Gotama passed into Nirvana, have I ever met a man, with the exception of Siddhartha, about whom I have felt the same. Siddhartha, he is a holy man! His ideas may be strange, and his words may sound foolish, but his glance, his hands, his skin, and his hair all radiate a purity, peace, serenity, gentleness, and saintliness. I have never seen this kind of holy radiation in any man since the recent death of our illustrious teacher."

While Govinda was confused by his disordered thoughts and while there was a conflict in his heart, he, once again filled with affection, bowed to Siddhartha. He bowed low before the quietly seated man.

"Siddhartha," said Govinda, "we are now old men. We may never see each other again in this life. I can see, my dear friend, that you have found peace. I, however, realize that I have not yet found it. Tell me one more word, my esteemed friend, tell me something that I can conceive and tell me something that I can understand. Give me something to help me on my way, Siddhartha. My path is often hard and dark."

Siddhartha was silent and looked at Govinda with his calm, peaceful smile.

Govinda looked steadily at the Siddhartha's face with anxiety and with longing. Suffering, continual seeking, and continual failure together were clearly written in his look.

Siddhartha saw what was disclosed on Govinda's look and smiled.

"Bend near to me!" Siddhartha whispered into the Govinda's ear. "Come, still nearer, quite close! Kiss me on my forehead, Govinda!"

Even though it was a surprise, Govinda was compelled by a great love and the presentiment to obey his friend. He leaned close to Siddhartha and touched Siddhartha's forehead with his lips. As he kissed Siddhartha's forehead, something wonderful happened to him. While his thoughts were still dwelling on Siddhartha's strange words, while he was still striving in vain to dispel the conception of time, while his mind was still struggling fruitlessly to imagine Nirvana and Samsara as one, and while a certain contempt for his friend's words was still conflicting with a tremendous love and esteem inside him, this something wonderful happened to him.

Now, he no longer saw the face of his friend Siddhartha. Instead, he saw other faces, many faces, a long series of faces, a continuous stream of faces, hundreds of thousands of faces. Together, they came all of a sudden and disappeared all of a sudden, but at the same time, they all seemed to be there. They all continually changed and incessantly renewed themselves; however, all these new faces were just Siddhartha.

He saw the face of a fish and the face of a carp with tremendous painfully opened mouths. He saw the face of a dying fish with a pair of tear-dimmed eyes. He saw the face of a newly born child, a red face filled with wrinkles, ready to cry. He saw the face of a murderer and saw him plunging a knife into the body of a man. At the same moment, he saw this same murderer kneeling down, being held in chains, and then being decapitated by an executioner. He saw the naked bodies of men and women in the postures and in the excessive enthusiasm of passionate love. He saw corpses that were stretched out, stiff, cold, and empty. He saw the heads of different animals—panthers, crocodiles, elephants, oxen, and birds. He saw Krishna, known as the preserver God of Creation, and Agni, known as the God of fire and the Acceptor of sacrifices for onwards conveyance to other deities. He saw all these forms and all these faces in thousands of thousands of relationships to each other.

They all helped each other and loved each other, but at the same time, they all also hated each other and destroyed each other. Finally, they all became newly reborn. Each form was eventually led to death that was just a passionate, painful example of ephemerality. Yet, none of them died. They only transformed from one form to another. They were always reborn and continually had a new face in each new cycle. Only did time stand between one face and another. All these forms and faces rested, flowed, reproduced, swam past, and merged into each other. And over all these forms and faces, there was a continually something which was thin, unreal, and yet existing stretching across. This continually something was like a thin glass-like layer, like a sheet of ice, and like a transparent skin and played a role as if it was a shell, a form, or a mask of water. This mask of water, overall, was Siddhartha's smiling face that Govinda kissed with his lips at that moment.

And Govinda saw that this mask-like smile, this smile of unity over the flowing forms, this smile of simultaneousness over the thousands of births and deaths—this smile of Siddhartha—was, indeed, exactly the same as the calm, delicate, impenetrable, perhaps gracious, perhaps mocking, wise thousand-fold smile of Gotama, the Buddha that he, himself, had perceived it a hundred times with awe. The smile was in such a manner, Govinda knew, that the Perfect One smiled.

No longer knowing whether time existed or not, whether this eyesight had lasted a second or a hundred years, whether this person was Siddhartha or Gotama, and whether in this individual was a *Self* or something else, it appeared that Govinda was just deeply wounded by a divine arrow which pleased him, enchanted him, and exalted him. Overwhelmingly, Govinda stood still for a little while, but he remained bent over Siddhartha's peaceful face, which he just kissed and which just become the stage of all present and future forms.

Siddhartha's countenance remained unchanged after the mirror of the thousand-fold forms disappeared from the surface. He smiled peacefully and gently—perhaps very graciously and perhaps very mockingly, just exactly as the Illustrious One smiled.

Govinda bowed low while uncontrollable tears trickled down his old face. The feeling of great love and the feeling of the most humble veneration completely overwhelmed him. He bowed low, right down to the ground, in front of the motionless, sitting man whose smile reminded him of everything that he had ever loved in his life and of everything that he had ever regarded as valuable and holy in his life.

Remark: Siddhartha's sixth awakening—Resting in equanimity and remaining at tranquility regardless of whatever happened in life was Siddhartha's sixth awakening, Siddhartha's ultimate awakening. After recognizing that the great song of a thousand voices consisted of only the sacred sound "Om" and after accepting the inevitability that life was so, Siddhartha became awakened that there was no difference among numerous voices, and the stream of life events was the music of life.

.~.*·*·*.~.

If you like Siddhartha and are curious about potential insights hidden behind the story, please continue to entertain yourself with
Siddhartha's Insights.

Made in the USA
Lexington, KY
06 September 2017